Diane, 2— from! (handwritten)

From the
KITCHEN
to
the CORNER
OFFICE *Mom's Wisdom on Leadership*

Applying the Skills Motherhood Has Taught to Achieve Career Success

MICHELLE YOZZO DRAKE

Foreword by MARK VICTOR HANSEN *New York Times* Best-Selling Author
INTERIOR ILLUSTRATIONS by Pat Drake Snyder

Part of the MegaBook Series

NEW YORK

From the KITCHEN to the CORNER OFFICE

By Michelle Yozzo Drake

ISBN: 978-1-60037-381-7 Paperback

ISBN: 978-1-60037-380-0 Hardcover

Library of Congress Control Number: 2007940542

Part of the *MegaBook Series*
Published by:

MORGAN · JAMES
THE ENTREPRENEURIAL PUBLISHER™

Morgan James Publishing, LLC
1225 Franklin Ave Ste 325
Garden City, NY 11530-1693
Toll Free 800-485-4943
www.MorganJamesPublishing.com

Cover and Interior Design by:
Heather Kirk
www.GraphicsByHeather.com
Heather@GraphicsByHeather.com

Interior Illustrations by:
Pat Drake Snyder

Habitat
for Humanity®
Peninsula
Building Partner

DEDICATION

To all the amazing women in my life…

Especially to:

My mother, Ann Sherman Yozzo, whose playful, positive and faith-filled approach to life serves as a constant beacon of light guiding me. I thank God everyday for my blessings because of what you have taught me.

ACKNOWLEDGMENTS

This book would not exist without the encouragement, support, sacrifice and dedication of my husband and business partner Rich. Thank you for always pushing me to be my best and for putting some of your dreams on the sideline as I pursue mine…Are you ready for the ride?

Thank you to my sons, Michael and Kevin. The precious gift of motherhood has changed my world forever… I am so excited to see how you boys make your mark in the world. Know your mama loves you!!!

Thank you to my father, Frank Yozzo, for your constant belief in me and my ability.

Thank you to my mother, Ann Yozzo, and my mother-in-law, Marty Drake…you have both been the inspiration for this book concept! Thank you for the love and the lessons!

Thank you to my sisters, Julie, Sheila, and Kate and my sisters-in-law Laura, Terri, Pat, Marcia, Chrissy, Rainey, Charlotte, Jane, Sue, Lynn, Eileen, and Anne whose varied approaches to and interpretation of life's situations always help to broaden my perspective of who I am and how I fit into the world. There were many amazing stories about all of you that did not make it into this book…but there's always the next one!

A huge thanks goes out to my incredible team at the Cove Group and to all of the women I have been blessed to work with over the years. It is a privilege to be associated with each and every one of you. A special thanks needs to be noted to my assistant and project specialist, Rachel. Without your dedication, organization, creativity and commitment to supporting the ideas in my writing, radio show and online video show, none of it could get executed. Thank you!

Thanks go out to my amazing illustrator, Pat Drake Snyder. Thank you for adding to your stressful day by creating the visual manifestation of my written words. You are an amazing artist.

Thank you to my editor Dr. Patricia Ross, whose insights fine-tuned my words. Thank you to David Hancock and the team at Morgan James Publishing who made the process of publishing my first book a pleasure! Thank you to Mark Victor Hansen for writing my forward and believing in the importance of my message to working women across the globe.

Thank you to the hundreds of amazing women that I interviewed for this book. I wish that I could have included all of your stories in the Lipstick Leadership sections.

And finally, thank you to the amazing women in my life who have passed over. The memories of the lessons you taught me have shaped me into the woman I am today. Thank you Aunt Marie, for having been a kindred spirit, mentor, confidant, friend and the big sister I never had. I am thankful for the late-night girl talk sessions which fueled my creative expression and strength. Thank you Aunt Jennie, Aunt Ruthie and Mops for your examples in leadership, courage and faith, I will always remember your words and actions.

TESTIMONIALS

"Thank you for demystifying business, bread-making, and self confidence. Thank you for teaching me to put my fingers in paint, command an audience, raise my day-rate, and be unapologetic when I ask for what I want. My life has changed because of the precious gift of your time and energy. It is beautiful to see that you are sharing those same gifts with a global audience in the writing of this book, I loved it! How lucky we are to have your voice out in the world, a voice that will ring true to professional women everywhere."

~Shalini Kantayya, President of 7th Empire Media, New York City

"A master story-teller, Michelle couples inspiring and heartwarming stories of 'mother's wisdom' with practical, accessible, and real world leadership applications. By sharing the wisdom of mothers in a distinctly feminine tone, this book goes beyond the standard male-oriented leadership books to provide a unique voice that readers who are women professionals, managers and executives will find speaks to them and for them in a powerful way."

~Mark Victor Hansen, NY Times #1 Bestselling Author of the Chicken Soup for the Soul Series, Newport Beach

"I laughed, I cried, you made me think…just what I love in a book!"

~Dr. Patricia Ross, Denver

"From the Kitchen to the Corner Office is a treasure chest of wisdom and sage advice. What a delightful collection for stay-at-home moms and CEO's alike. While our experiences may differ, we've all received advice from other women throughout our lives. This book beautifully captures timeless lessons for us to pass along and groom the next generation of leaders."

~Kristen Marie Schuerlein, Founder and CEO, Affirmagy Inc., Seattle

"In a world where there's arguably too much information but not enough that truly informs, this book is an eye-opener."

~Regina Maruca, Former Editor for The Harvard Business Review *and co-author of* The Leadership Legacy, *Boston*

"Michelle's insightful book helped me rediscover and recognize all the essential tools I need (and have) to evolve without reinventing myself. The miracle of this book lies in its power to silence our doubts, embolden our esteem, and ultimately listen to the voice of our own intuition."

~Angela Gervasio, Vice President/Producer, Crew Creative Advertising, Los Angeles

FOREWORD

BY MARK VICTOR HANSEN, CO-AUTHOR OF THE
CHICKEN SOUP FOR THE SOUL SERIES

Motherhood is a magical, but sometimes exhausting experience. To date, society has overlooked the value of motherhood in relation to business. Now, with Michelle Yozzo Drake's brilliant new book, it can also be a money-making experience, transforming kitchen leadership into career savvy. What Michelle has done is taken motherhood in all of its blissful complexity and turned it into an income stream.

Women all over the globe have made their roles as mothers look effortless and are now discovering how to adapt these skills entrepreneurially. They are applying what motherhood has taught them about organization skills, financial planning, relationship building, problem solving and crisis management to achieve career success.

As this trend continues, it's time for women to bridge the gap between motherhood and work — and bring the wisdom and insights of motherhood into the workplace. The payoff for women is gaining the ability to be themselves at work — rather than trying to fit into the "man's world" environment — and leveraging their feminine wisdom as a tool for decision making, empowering workers and teams, and communication. The result for the workplace is the creation of healthier organizations that are growing, thriving, and meeting the needs of real people in a powerful new way — a paradigm shift that is long overdue.

I applaud Michelle's great work in helping all of us understand that the kitchen may be the best training ground for entrepreneurship and visionary leadership.

- Mark Victor Hansen

CONTENTS

Foreword by Mark Victor Hansen
   Co-author of the *Chicken Soup for the Soul* series xi

A Note from Michelle xvii

Chapter 1: *From the Kitchen to the Corner Office* 1
   Mommy Management Training 1
   Grab a Cup of Coffee 4
   Jumping Off the Building 7
   Mama Said! 12

Chapter 2: *Life is a Game...Play It!* 17
   American Royalty 17
   Today's Lesson: Fun! 18
   Thanksgiving Treasure Hunt 20
   The Hunt is On! 22
   Team Dynamics — Yozzo Style 25
      The Analysts: Michelle's Team 25
      The Tacticians: Julie's Team 26
      The Peacemakers: Sheila's Team 26
      The "Funsters": Pete and Kate's Team 27
   Whose Team Am I On? 29
   Team Building in the Woods .31

Time to Get Real 32

Mission Accomplished 33

MBA (Mom's Business Acumen) Class: It Pays to Play!
Getting More from Your Team 35

Chapter 3: *Stay Out of the Kitchen* 37

Meals with the Yozzos 37

Holidays — Italian Style 38

The Cooking History of Mimi and Marie 41

Aunt Marie's Feasts 42

Kitchen Leadership in the Boardroom 45

The Apprentice 48

Vying to be the Next *Apprentice* 49

Sean's Approach to Leadership .50

MBA (Mom's Business Acumen) Class: Tips for
Powerful Leadership 51

Chapter 4: *Toothpaste and Towels* 53

Mornings with Mimi 53

Nearby Town...Worlds Apart 56

The Strategy of a Hot Breakfast *and* a Hot Shower 60

The Cost-Saving Conundrum 61

Out with the Old 63

In with the New 65

MBA (Mom's Business Acumen) Class: What's Your System?
Seven Steps to Bringing Order to Your Chaos 68

Chapter 5: *Cleaning Habits of Little Boys* 71

    Mom Experience 71

    Balancing Work and Home .72

    New Kind of Window Cleaner 74

    Locked Out 76

    Daddy's Shingling Surprise .78

    But What Do You *Do?* 80

    Directing Your Team 81

    MBA (Mom's Business Acumen) Class: Getting Your
    Team Pulling Together 83

Chapter 6: *Wear Your Diamonds to the Beach* 85

    The Sherman History 85

    Golfing in the 1920s 87

    The Golfing "Socialite" 89

    Mops' Diamond Ring 90

    The Messenger Syndrome 93

    Letting "Diamond" Ideas Shine 93

    Pitching to the Boss 95

    MBA (Mom's Business Acumen) Class: Tips to Pitch
    Your Idea 96

Chapter 7: *Big Sister, Little Mom* 99

    The Woman in the Shoe 99

    What is Normal? 100

    Dinner with the Drakes 101

Chores at the Drake House 103

A Leader Emerges 105

A Little Boy's Memories 106

Pat's Leadership Style 110

Being a Coach-in-Law 111

From Teacher to Assistant Director 112

Moving Up in the Council 114

MBA (Mom's Business Acumen) Class: Cultivating
Power Contacts and Connections 115

Chapter 8: *It's Just Fine* 117

Skiing with Mimi 117

The Five-Second Rule 119

More Living to Do 120

A Big Decision 123

The Bumpy Flight 123

Networking at 30,000 Feet 124

Corporate Client #1 126

MBA (Mom's Business Acumen) Class: Choosing
Your Reality 127

Chapter 9: *Who Are You Talking to?* 133

Getting to Know You...Getting to Know All About You . . .133

Michelle, The Artist 134

Rich, The Process Guy 136

The Artist and the Process Guy at Work 138

Polar Opposites 139

Boating with the Boys 141

Marketing to *YOU!* 144

The Panel Interview 145

    Analyzing the Competition 146

    Analyzing the Interview Panel 146

    The Last Steps 150

Panel Results 153

MBA (Mom's Business Acumen) Class: The Four
Main Communication Styles 153

Chapter 10: *Stand Up* 157

Picture of Me 157

"Can't" Isn't a Word 158

Tragedy in New York 161

Overcoming Fear 163

My Professional Persona 165

Finding Power in My Art 166

The Artist's Coaching Process 170

New Fears to Overcome 173

MBA (Mom's Business Acumen) Class: Managing
Your Fear Checklist 175

Chapter 11: Becoming the Family Bread Maker 179

Bread Baking History 179

The First Lesson 181

Solo Mission 185

Just Like Aunt Jennie's! 187

Mentoring…Aunt Jennie Style 192

Immediate Connection 193

Mentoring the Filmmaker 196

Standing Ovation 197

On the Lot 198

MBA (Mom's Business Acumen) Class: Guideline
for Mentor-Mentee Relationships 199

Chapter 12: *Who's in **Your** Kitchen?* .201

Cortland Aunts and Uncles 201

Support from the Cortland Family 203

Coffee and Negotiation Strategies 205

Clamoring for Coaching 206

Get Your M.B.A. (Mom's Business Acumen) Today 208

About the Author 213

A NOTE FROM MICHELLE

Dear Reader,

Have you ever sat in a business meeting and heard your mother's voice come flying out of your mouth! This book is about listening to that voice, even if it frightens you! For it's the wisdom of our mothers and all the female figures in our lives that will guide us to the success we desire and deserve

Congratulations! You are about to embrace what it means to be a **Woman in Charge** and to learn how the simple truths of "Mom knows best" can be applied in the workplace!

We, as women, have a collection of tools we bring to the workplace, but they are tools we haven't really explored in depth. We acquire these tools doing what we have done for centuries. It is no great revelation that women have run the organization that has been the backbone of this country for generations — THE FAMILY! If you study this organization that we call 'the family', you will note it has been full of restructuring and downsizing over the years. It has been though a lot of cultural changes, but one of the constants has been the matriarch and her feminine leadership.

We really need to learn to own our talents and our skills as mothers and wives. Our feminine perspective brings our best into the workplace, and it can help us achieve power, prestige and prosperity.

Women are emerging as leaders of corporations, small businesses, educational institutions and non-profit organizations. As more of the Baby Boomer men meet the age of retirement, the number of women leaders is going to increase dramatically! Gone are the days where women are only coming into organizations at entry level positions. Women are running organizations. They're senior managers and working with diverse groups of people. Women lead these people, motivate them, and bring out the best in them. They do more, and they do it with less money, better time management, and more finesse. To most women, these highly desirable management skills are second nature because they do these things all the time at home, running the family organization, without even really thinking about it.

Because women are a major component in the workplace, they now hold down two MAJOR CAREERS as they balance their responsibilities as CEO of the family with outside work. It's not that the men aren't important, but women have traditionally had to juggle a lot of different roles and work harder than ever in order to get an opportunity in the workplace. To take advantage of those opportunities, we have to draw from our greatest source of success: running our households and families. From that area of our lives, there are many lessons we can learn and take into that workplace.

The feminine perspective differs historically and genetically from a traditional male perspective in business. The male perspective has traditionally been very transactional. However, the female perspective is relational. Women are typically more relationship-oriented, and because success in business is largely due to building relationships and communities, women have a lot to offer! For example, in management roles, you need motivated people to actually get the work done and encourage your team to grow in their skill sets. As mothers, we've got tons of experience doing this. We're constantly nurturing strengths in our children.

The chapters that follow talk about the female perspective on leadership and how it applies in the workplace. Anyone who's had to convince a child it was bedtime, convince a teenager they shouldn't go out and drink with buddies, or convince their daughter that their relationship with a friend is toxic knows the negotiation skills you develop and use at home can also be utilized in the workplace.

This book focuses on how I have used in my business all the lessons from all the important women in my life; each chapter has a personal story from the home and a case study of how the "simple truth" of the story can be applied in a work situation. Accompanying these tales are the "Lipstick Leadership" sections, stories and quotes from the hundreds of professional women I have interviewed for my radio show and worked with over the years. Each chapter ends with exercises and tips called "MBA (Mom's Business Acumen) Class" that include actions you can take at work to apply Mom's wisdom.

In my role as a woman at work, I'm a unique blend of traditional and modern. I've had a very traditional Italian upbringing, and I view myself in a very traditional role in my home. However, I am also the CEO of a management and marketing corporation! I have personally gone from the kitchen to the corner office, and I've helped others do the same thing because my company helps to coach, manage and train executives on how to move their careers forward and entrepreneurs on how to build their dream. What I found in working with hundreds of women executives —

and from the women I interviewed for this book — was the skills they developed or acquired as mothers or from their mothers, grandmothers, sisters, or girlfriends are the traits that propelled them into the leadership roles they have today.

This book is about being aware of your own skills and of all of the different ways we can nurture them and bring them powerfully into the world of work. Its underlying theme is to help you find the ability to embrace and be comfortable with who we are and what we have to offer. This is simply how our lives feel complete.

There have been wonderful women in my life who have helped to mold and cultivate me into the woman I am today. And personally and professionally I LIKE THE WOMAN I AM TODAY! So thank you, Mom, for all the times you gave me your advice — even if I acted like I did not need it or want it…you stuck with me!

Today we start to embrace the simple truths from Mom that can help drive your career!

The Simple Truth from Mom: She always knows best!

Learn the secrets of the board room big shots…the ones they don't want you to know! Secrets about advancing your career, building a high performance team, creating strategic initiatives to improve productivity, and more are REVEALED in my CEOSecretBlueprint.com program.

For a LIMITED TIME, readers can get my CEO Secret Blueprint E-Course (valued at $279) as my FREE gift to you. Simply go to CEOSecretBlueprint.com today and enter the code K2CO to get started.

CHAPTER 1

FROM THE KITCHEN TO THE CORNER OFFICE

MOMMY MANAGEMENT TRAINING

Surviving the "Mommy Management Training Program" is not for the faint of heart. It is a training program that expects its manager to deliver immediately. It's the kind of program that doesn't give you a lot of time to learn how; it forces you to learn on the job...while trying not to screw it up too badly.

Since I have never actually seen them written down, I thought I would provide you with the "Mommy Management Training Program" rules. As I have come to know them, they are:

1. No sick days

2. No holidays

3. On-call 24/7

4. No training manual

5. Here's the baby…good luck!

The lessons that have come from my stint in the "Mommy Management Training Program" have helped to position me for success as the CEO of a management consulting firm, and I believe those skills translate into insights for success in many different kinds of jobs.

As women, we have been leading groups of people for years. Some of the most dynamic leaders I've been exposed to have come from unlikely sources. They are women who, if you ask them, "Are you a leader?" might not know what you're talking about. These women have limited work experience outside the home but the greatest work ethic I've ever observed. They are the greatest managers, negotiators and salespeople I've ever met. We all know these women. They are our mothers, our sisters, our grandmothers, our mothers-in-law and even our daughters. They are dynamic leaders because motherhood and the nurturing of families is truly the greatest management training program any woman could experience.

Now, actually being a mom is helpful but not required. Having a mother or a mother-figure play a prominent role in your life gives you the working model off of which to jump to have a successful career. Think about the skills demonstrated over the years as women successfully groomed their *home teams*: their children, spouse, in-laws, parents, and siblings. Those same skills guarantee success in the workplace, too.

Years ago, it was common for the matriarch to not only manage her immediate family but also her extended family as well. Times may have changed since then and the "nuclear" family has shrunk in size, but the lessons from those old-fashioned kitchens remain relevant in modern culture — especially in the workplace. Today's woman needs to draw on the wisdom of the dynamic "kitchen" leaders of the past in order to find success now and in the future, and this is the book that will guide them to that success through its stories and exercises.

Lipstick Leadership

"[There is] one thing that stands out in my mind that Mom used to say to us years ago (and still would today given the chance...I find myself using this and passing it on to my kids all the time, too!). You know how you wake up on a cold winter day with a sore throat from the heat and a stuffy nose and just basically feeling rotten? Mom used to always say: "Get up and get moving and you'll feel fine." I would never believe it at

that moment because I was sure I was dying from the flu, but sure enough, I'd get up, get in the shower and by the time I'm driving to work, I feel mostly fine.

Thanks to Mom's advice, I've made it to work more days than not and now I say it to my kids all the time. I sometimes wonder if Mom hadn't said that to me so many years ago on such a regular basis, if as a working person today, would I just give in to my sore throat, call in sick and go back to sleep? My employer should call my mom and thank her! I have a few employees I'd like to give Mom's number to, too!!"

~ Kathryn Gaddis, Recreation Superintendent,
  Ocean City Park and Recreation

**Submit your best "Mom's Wisdom" story at
www.LipstickLeadership.com today!**

GRAB A CUP OF COFFEE

When I think of my mother Mimi's kitchen, I remember a playful but productive atmosphere where everyone had a job to do. During the holiday preparations, you would enter the kitchen and find a cloud of flour dust hovering in the air, mixing with the sounds of chatter and laughter and the most amazing smells. The aroma of the kitchen was a strange yet tantalizing blend of apple pie, chicken soup, tomato sauce and cooking meat — staples in our holiday meals. Looking over at the counter, you would see my sisters making salad and appetizers, cookies and mashed potatoes. And you would find me making the wonderful bread my Aunt Jennie was famous for. On the floor level, you would notice our helpers, the grandchildren, each with a special project of their own — usually a scaled down version of whatever their mom was working on. Being in the kitchen, we were always surrounded by a communal atmosphere full of banter as we put final touches on the meal for our families to enjoy.

My mother's talent for engaging "help" in the kitchen was not limited to just my family. I remember one afternoon when I was in high school. I had just finished my after-school practice for the varsity tennis team and walked into my mother's kitchen to find six of my best guy friends getting a lesson in making homemade pizza from my mother. My mother attracts people of all ages to her and to her table. When she sends a dinner invitation, there's never a "Sorry, I can't make it," reply because everyone knows they would be missing out on something very special.

So today I'm happy to invite YOU into my mother's kitchen to listen to the stories and lessons I've learned from my mother and from the many women sitting at her kitchen table. Welcome! Each amazing woman in my family and in my life has given me different tools to use at work, and each of the chapters in this book is dedicated to those lessons. I'm excited for you to meet:

◆ My mother Mimi, the expert in bringing a team together and motivating them;

- ◆ My Aunt Marie, an authority on organization and communication;

- ◆ My grandmother Mops, a role model for building confidence and timing;

- ◆ My sister-in-law Pat, a master at influencing from within an organization;

- ◆ My mother-in-law Marty, a pro at creating order from chaos;

- ◆ My Great Aunt Jennie, the most incredible mentor I've ever known;

- ◆ My children and husband, the surprising teachers who've helped in preparing me to be the CEO of the Cove Group, through my experience as a mother and wife.

By tapping into the wisdom of my mother and the female role models in my life on communication, creativity, rewarding exceptional behavior and leading teams, I have had a tremendous influence in the workplace. I've moved myself into positions of power and leadership.

It's an exhilarating time to be a woman and to be in a management role. Gone are the days where we have to act like a man in order to be successful in the workplace — and that's exciting to me! Now we can share our feminine perspective and be the leaders the world needs!

But from where do we draw the strength necessary to become powerful leaders? For me, the journey to discover that strength began with an unconventional final exam and the voices of my mother, aunts and grandmother whispering in my head.

Lipstick Leadership

"My mother ingrained in me the importance of a prompt, nicely-written thank you note. This habit, while simple, has served me well in business—mainly because so many people neglect to express their gratitude for things"

~ Rochelle Kopp, Managing Principal, Japan Intercultural Consulting

Advance your career with the help of Michelle's FREE e-zine. Sign up today at www.LipstickLeadership.com!

JUMPING OFF THE BUILDING

When I was in college I had a defining moment, a moment in time when I was able to see not only who I was, but who I could become — a leader — if I was brave enough to conquer my fears.

I was a business major, and as a freshman, I had a statistics class that met at 8:30 in the morning. I had a difficult time getting to class because the freedom of college and the variety of options for activities at night kept me out late and made it a struggle to get up in the morning for class. After a few weeks of sleeping through my alarm and missing class, I turned to my skill as an analytical problem solver to remedy the situation. I knew I needed to do something before I ended up failing the class. You know, classes cost big money whether you pass or fail!

So I dropped the statistics class, and I picked up a class in leadership that, as luck would have it, was only a ten-week course that started three weeks after the semester began. Looking at the description, I thought I would be studying different leaders and leadership styles and maybe take a few tests and write a paper or two that drew conclusions about what made them strong. I could do that! And it met at 10:00 a.m. which was perfect! I knew I was making the right choice…what I didn't know was the class department letters **ROTC** meant **Reserve Officer Training Corp.!**

On the first day of class, I was bewildered to find that instead of meeting inside a regular building, the class convened in an unusual looking structure behind the buildings. A ROTC hut is what I quickly learned it was called. As I took my place at one of the tables, I noticed all of my classmates were boys, most of whom I'd never even seen before. I was a popular girl and had made friends with all sorts of people — where had these guys been hiding, I wondered.

When the instructor made his way to the front of the hut, that's when I *really* got nervous. He was dressed in a full military uniform! He introduced himself in a stern booming voice and demanded we call him "Captain." When he explained this was a Reserve Officer Training Corp. class, my stomach dropped into my shoes.

"This class is going to turn you boys into men," Captain barked, obviously failing to notice the blond girl in the baby blue sweater seated before him. "We're going to learn about leadership the military way. And don't bother with fancy clothes for this class, just comfortable shoes and something you won't mind getting muddy."

Boys into men…the military way…MUDDY?!

What in the world had I gotten myself into?

After class I raced back to my room to review my options. Unfortunately, the final date to drop classes and still receive a refund had just passed. If I tried to drop the class now, not only would I lose money, I would be short on credits for the semester, and I couldn't afford either. So whether I liked it or not, I was stuck with the Captain and military training once a week for an entire semester.

I showed up at the next class still hopeful: "Maybe it won't be so bad…" I thought. At 10 a.m. sharp — or 0:10:00 hundred hours — the Captain strolled into the ROTC hut, wasted no time on pleasantries, and ordered us to follow him outside. He led us to the wooded area at the end of campus and simply said, "Five mile run. Ready…GO!" and we took off, sprinting through the mud. Even though I was in good shape, soon I was gulping down air like it was going out of style, but I refused to slow down and show my all-male classmates I couldn't compete with them.

The following weeks of class were just as grueling as I feared they'd be, but I held my own and pushed past the pain and fear. We ran those five miles often, and when we weren't running, there were plenty of other ways the Captain — or "Captain Evil" as I secretly referred to him — could torture us.

He took us to the rifle range where we learned to shoot guns. I would stand there holding one, swaying back and forth — they were so heavy a gust of wind could've knocked me over. I called on all of my strength to hoist the gun up to eye level, and just before I pulled the trigger, I'd have to squeeze my eyes shut and turn my head away! The recoil nearly knocked me on my rear more than once and always left me with a sore shoulder. I thought I just wasn't cut out for gunplay until Captain taught us about supine shooting: lying on your stomach with the gun propped on the ground. I was great at **that**! In fact, I was the best in my class!

Captain also took us to the obstacle course many times. He proved he wasn't entirely evil when he didn't make us complete it on our introduction to it. Instead, he divided the course among a few classes. Each class we would tackle another aspect of it: running through tires, swinging on a rope over a mud pit, and climbing up a fifteen foot wall. After we'd gone through each piece separately, the following class he made us go through the entire thing and timed us — and this was after our five mile run!

A few classes into the semester, I began wondering about my grade. How can you really assign a letter grade to running or shooting? Every class I would ask him: "How are we going to get graded?" He flashed his evil grin — the same one I'd seen before he ordered us to run and climb and swing — and said, "Wait until the final. The final will determine your grade."

When I arrived at the ROTC hut on the day of the final, there was a note on the door. "Cadets: Report to the top floor of the Science Building for your final exam." Finally! We would be sitting in a real classroom and taking a real test. I exhaled in relief. I knew I could ace an essay or two describing this very unique educational experience that was ROTC Leadership 101!

I headed over to the Science Building and climbed the stairs to the very top. I opened the door and…felt a warm breeze. I was on the roof! Surely I made a mistake, I thought, and then I saw the rest of my class and Captain. In his hands were ropes and harnesses, and he explained our final exam was jumping off the building!!!

"You have two options," he roared. "Jump off the building and rappel down the side, and you get an A for the class. Don't jump off the building, and you FAIL. Any questions? No. Good. Who's up first?" The boys eagerly lined up, and they were excited and laughing. I stood there weighing my options. It would certainly seem like an easy decision: jump and get an A or don't and get an F and have wasted an entire semester playing with guns and guys. However, I am afraid of heights; severely afraid of heights…sometime even high heels freak me out! How could I jump off a ten story building??

I decided there must be some other way. As the boys jumped off the side of the building, I approached the Captain. I put on my most miserable face and said, "Captain? I don't think I can jump because I'm very afraid of heights. What if I wrote an essay instead?" He stared me down and yelled, "I told you, cadet, you have only two options and writing an essay isn't one of them! Now get over there and *jump off this building!*"

After trying unsuccessfully to reason with him, I have to confess I pulled out every shameful girl trick I could think of to get out of jumping. First I tried crying. Most men can't resist a crying woman, but Captain was unmoved. He screamed at me again, "Get over there and jump off this building, cadet!!" I tried begging next, "Please, Captain. I'm so scared, and I just can't do it. Please don't make me, please!" His loud response was the same.

As the last boy jumped off the side, I tried playing the sick card. "I swear, Captain, if I have to stand on that ledge and jump, I'm going to faint…or-or I'll be sick! I'll be sick all over the place!" He shouted at me again and said, "It won't bother me if you get sick, cadet! The only people it'll bother are those boys down there are on the ground waiting for you to *jump off this building!*" I stole a glance at the door, wondering if I could possibly outrun him and speed down the stairs to the ground. He caught my look and yelled, "You can't outrun me, cadet, so don't even think about it!"

MAMA SAID!

Finally, he and I were alone on the roof, him bellowing at me and me crying and pleading. I was out of options and just stood there helplessly. Then the Captain stopped in mid-scream. He looked at me with a thoughtful expression on his face, and to my surprise, he suddenly crouched down to my level and spoke to me a calm, gentle voice. "You can do this, cadet. I know you can do this. I believe in you. I've watched you hold your own against these boys. I know you can do this. You can push past this fear because you're strong."

When he finished speaking and we stood there in the quiet, his voice echoing in my brain, I started to hear other voices from my past.

My mother's voice: *Make it a game, Shelly. Pretend it's an adventure. You can do this!*

My Great Aunt Jennie's broken English: *Michelina, you already have everything you need inside to do this!*

My grandmother Mops' stern voice: *Bring your A-game. A woman can do this — look at all I've accomplished!*

And finally my Aunt Marie: *You know when to lead and how to follow. Follow the Captain, and he'll lead you to yourself.*

I looked into Captain Evil's not so evil eyes and saw he believed I could get past my fear; he believed in me. In the end, Captain Evil was Captain Empowerment! I took the harness and rope from his hands, hooked myself in, and stepped up onto the edge of the roof. I let my heels hang over the side, and when I looked down, I felt a flutter of nausea and the more powerful feeling of *I can do this.* The boys at the bottom looked up and me and started yelling out encouragement. I took a deep breath and *jumped off the building!*

To an onlooker it must've been quite a sight: a blond girl wearing hot pink corduroy pants hanging down the side of a building! I rappelled quickly, keeping my eyes on the wall in front of me and trying to follow the old adage: "Don't look down!" And then I felt my feet touch the solid ground. I unhooked myself and stood there, a little wobbly but amazed at what I had done. The feeling I had as I looked back up at the building was a feeling of power that has since been unmatched. I knew at that moment I could do anything. I knew whatever life would throw at me, I would have the strength to do what ever I needed to do to be successful. Pretty incredible that just jumping off that building could give me a moment of such clarity about who I am!

By being able to overcome my fear, I started to know I could trust myself. I had that defining moment in time where I got to see everything I could be later on in my life; it was a picture drawn by the women who believed in me, triggered by a passionate instructor, and executed by the woman I was becoming.

I've drawn upon that experience repeatedly over the past twenty-seven years with knowledge that I have the tools to overcome fear. So when I'm afraid of the interview, the relationship, the new job, or the new client, I remember, *I jumped off a building.*

Lipstick Leadership

"My grandmother taught me that a woman can be powerful by her very presence, even when she's embroidering flowered tablecloths. Although my grandmother didn't have a corner office, she had her corner of the living room from which she exuded as much power as a top CEO!"

~ Carole Lieberman, M.D., Beverly Hills psychiatrist/ author/talk show host

Submit your best "Mom's Wisdom" story at www.LipstickLeadership.com today!

That knowledge helped me overcome a violent physical attack I survived because I was able to manage my fear. It helped me overcome the loss of my best friend in a plane crash. It helped me overcome major illness. It helped me overcome failing at certain aspects of my business early on. And it helps guide me on a daily basis as CEO of The Cove Group, Inc.

The ability to know you can get past the failures and you can get past the fear gives you a level of comfort in taking risks in your life you might not have taken. It has kept me from becoming complacent. The main reason I was able to jump off of that building is because of the lessons my mother, my grandmother, and my aunts taught me. I'm excited to share those lessons with you, but I'm more excited to get you thinking about the stories from your life. You may not have realized the women in your life who taught you valuable lessons can give you what you need to advance your career today!

Want help and guidance to improve your management skills and get you positioned for earning more money? Well, I want to help! Join me at CEOSecretBlueprint.com, and I'll share the secrets that years of executive coaching have taught me...lessons that can now help YOU!

For a LIMITED TIME my introductory e-course is FREE to my readers. Just enter the code K2CO to get started with your coaching session. COME ON! WHAT ARE YOU WAITING FOR...JUMP!

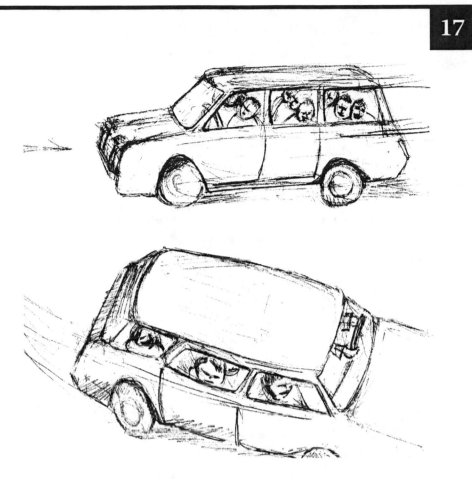

CHAPTER 2

LIFE IS A GAME...PLAY IT!

AMERICAN ROYALTY

My parents met in college, and they were an unlikely couple from the start. My father hailed from New York City, the son of Italian immigrants, and was raised in a boisterous household. My mother, a descendant of one of the founding families of our country, grew up with a very proper upbringing. This unique combination of cultural heritages made my family an interesting mixture of perspectives, traditions and experiences.

My mom, Mimi, grew up as Gertrude Ann Sherman in an upstate New York home so vast it could have housed a small town within it! As descendants of U.S. Vice-President James Schoolcraft Sherman, generations of her family lived in this spectacular home until my grandmother sold it in 1965 after the death of my grandfather. I remember the house well; it was a massive four-story building topped with turrets that reminded me of Cinderella's castle. It lay at the top of a hill overlooking the town and a sprawling lawn and seventy-one rooms made it perfect for games of hide and seek when we visited!

Mimi was one of three children; her sister Catherine was artistic, her brother Jim was a musician, and she was the athlete. My grandfather, Pops, encouraged these talents in his children. All Mimi needed to do was mention at dinner that she shot arrows in gym class and Pops would come home the next night with everything needed for an archery range to entertain her. Pops owned a hardware and sporting goods store with his older sisters and mother, so Mimi grew up playing all sorts of sports, including field hockey, golf, curling, softball, basketball, track, and even girls ice hockey! Her childhood was filled with fun and games, so it is no surprise she has made several careers out of having fun.

TODAY'S LESSON: FUN!

With her down-to-earth personality, Mimi never put on airs or dreamed of life in high society. She earned a teaching degree in college with a certification in physical education. Before I was born, she taught high school Phys. Ed. and after she started having kids, she put her career on hold to stay home with us. Once we were all old enough for school, she returned to work; I was a teenager by then, and my youngest sister Kate is nine years younger than I am. Mom chose to teach nursery school and spend her days playing with and teaching the little kids. She didn't want to come home to us, burnt out from the problems of teenagers only to face more teenage problems. So she traded teenage hormones, problems with boys and attitudes for Play Dough, hopscotch and shoe-tying! It was the perfect balance for both Mom and us!

Lipstick Leadership

"Most everything I learned about work and work ethic, I learned from my father. The most important woman in my life was my grandmother. She taught me many, many things about gardens, animals and birds, and unconditional love — but not about work. On reflection, that probably was the best lesson to learn...work isn't everything."

~ Chris Chrissos, Political Aide

Advance your career with the help of Michelle's FREE e-zine. Sign up today at www.LipstickLeadership.com!

Mimi's teaching career focused on FUN: a key element of my mother's personality and a requirement for her curriculum. And she often brought her "work" home with her, especially during the holidays. With such a large extended family, we alternated the location of the holidays between my family's home and my father's sister Marie's home. Mimi and Aunt Marie would usually have the week before the holiday together to prepare... and entertain nine children. It's no wonder they got into the habit of playing games with us!

THANKSGIVING TREASURE HUNT

One Thanksgiving when my siblings, cousins and I were all grown with children of our own, Mimi orchestrated a game that topped those of past holidays: The Yozzo Memory Lane Treasure Hunt. She wanted to entertain us as well as take us on a walk down memory lane with childhood memories. When my father Pop -Pop questioned how this would be any fun for the in-laws and grandchildren, Mimi told him the team leaders — her children — would make telling the story behind the clue fun for everyone on their team — all twenty-five of us!

After we ate our homemade antipasto, soup, and pasta courses, my mother left the table and returned with a basket. Inside were little pieces of paper, one for every single person in our family. She then asked me, my sisters Julie, Sheila and Katie and my brother Peter to go stand in the front yard, leaving the in-laws and grandchildren sitting at the dinner table. Obedience trumped curiosity, and we marched outside. Mimi proceeded to pull names from the basket, dividing up the family into four teams. Our teams stood there, uncertain what we were going to be asked to do next and wondering what kind of crazy game our mother had dreamed up this year!

With the teams organized, Mimi then assigned each one a vehicle, a first for a holiday game. She then announced, "There is a treasure hidden somewhere here in town, the town where you all grew up. It's your job to find that treasure. This hunt is a walk down memory lane, and whoever has the best memory will win the treasure! The clues make reference to things that happened in the history of our family and are hidden across the whole town. Each clue will lead you to the next and one step closer to the treasure. Each team will be given a different first clue. The first team that finds the treasure gets to keep it. Good luck!"

The rules of the game were simple:

1. When the porch bell rings, get your team into your assigned car.

2. The Team Captain is the driver.

3. Buckle-up all team members.

4. Once buckled, read your first clue — it's waiting on the steering wheel.

5. Proceed to the clue site.

6. ALL team members must get out of the car and move to the clue location.

7. Pick up the clue...but don't read it yet!

8. The entire team must return to the car.

9. Go back to rule 3.

Repeat until you find the treasure!!! Good luck and PLAY the GAME!!!

And then the bell rang!

THE HUNT IS ON!

There was chaos everywhere as we all scrambled to our assigned cars. My team consisted of my brother-in-law John, who grew up in Maryland and was the most recent addition to the family; my oldest son, nine-year-old Michael; and my four-year-old nephew Matt. John and I buckled up the kids in my mini-van and read the first clue. It was about me, a lucky break!

> *A tear from Mommy and from me*
> *The door closes on Shelle,*
> *She's growing up you'll see*

I peeled out of the driveway, and in the rearview mirror, I caught a glimpse of Michael's eyes widening. I think he was a little shocked at how serious his mother was taking this competition, but Mimi brought us up to be game players! I didn't want to lose to any of my younger sisters or brother, so the competitor in me kicked in, and it was like I was fifteen-years-old again, playing football out in the front yard.

I quickly figured out the answer to the first clue. Mimi was referring to the entrance to my kindergarten...the *original* entrance. Two years after I went to kindergarten, the entrance to the building changed, and only the *new* entrance was familiar to Julie, the next sister in the clan to go to kindergarten. This gave us a jump! We all raced across the parking lot, through the playground to the doors of the kindergarten where we found our next clue hidden in the door jam! We raced back to the car, buckled in and read the scrap of paper, another poem-clue from Mom!

Bees are buzzing all around,
I'm not touching that sticky ground!

My parents owned an Italian ice stand called "Poppa Mia's Ice House" that we all had worked at during some point of our lives (fortunately for those of us who love free Italian ice, my sister Sheila took over ownership of the business and we have a new generation of Yozzo scoopers!). As I drove to the Ice House, I realized again, I had the advantage over a sibling: my brother Peter was an NCAA Division One Champion college athlete so he wrestled competitively in the summer, leaving no time for him to scoop Italian ice and move the sticky cans. I knew he would be dumbfounded by this clue, giving Team Michelle another leg up on the competition. We found the next clue wedged between the empty cans that lived with the bees behind the Ice House.

Winter or summer
It's a great place to go.
The little house on the island,
You know!

With the whole team in tow, I drove us to another location: the park. In the center of its pond was a gazebo with a dock linking it to the shore. During the heat of the summer, the family would picnic in the park and stand on the dock feeding the ducks. Frosty winters meant a frozen pond and plenty of ice skating. Sure enough, hidden in the gazebo was our next clue:

Hop on the boat, let's go to the beach.
If we had to swim, it would be a reach!

For years, my family lived on a boat at the beach during the summers when my parents, both teachers, had time off from work. We would take the boat over to Fire Island and live on it all summer; coming off it every two weeks to do laundry and grocery shop. When I was a teenager, we sold the boat and my parents bought a motor home, forcing us to take the ferry over to the beach. My team and I raced to the docks where we used to purchase our ferry tickets, and we found another clue:

> A *friendly* place for friends to meet,
> The competition is oh, so sweet.
> Everyone on your team must get a treat!

That could only mean the local Friendly's restaurant and ice cream shop where my siblings and I had spent much of our teenage years hanging out with friends. When we arrived, my team and I had to actually go inside and order ice cream before the kid behind the register would give us a clue! Small cones were handed out before I rushed everyone back into the minivan. As the mother of two driving a van littered with Cheerios, crayons and empty juice boxes, I could care less about the mess. Unfortunately for my sister Sheila and her team, her insistence that everyone eat their ice cream at Friendly's (instead of in her beautiful new car) meant lots of wasted time while the rest of us raced toward the finish line!

All afternoon, the teams raced across Sayville, trying to figure out clues and beat the other teams to the treasure. Despite my team's best effort, my sister Julie's team was the winner. Her team got to this final clue first:

Find the treasure...it is gold.
It's near Pop-Pop's favorite hole.

The treasure was buried in the backyard — right where we all started this hunt! Julie's team dug into the practice golf green my father constructed in the "way-back yard" where he practiced putting and chipping, and they found a small bag of coins, a treasure for the team to share.

They weren't the only ones to enjoy in a treasure. We all got to eat the next course of Mom's amazing food, and as we ate, we all laughed and shared how each team approached the treasure hunt. We started to compare notes on how each of us found the clues, and the business strategist in me found it interesting how the personalities and skill sets of each of the adult team members played a big role in how we played the game.

TEAM DYNAMICS — YOZZO STYLE

Each team definitely had its own perspective on how they worked with the clues they were given. All of the Yozzo kids were groomed by our game-playing mother and coach father to be competitive. We take our games seriously, and we want to win! In between taunting other teams from our cars and trying not to get speeding tickets, we worked through the clues and drew upon the talents within our teams to solve them, creating one of the best holiday memories in our family's history. Our teams could be characterized as follows:

The Analysts: Michelle's Team

In my car was my sister Kate's husband, John, an elementary school principal who grew up in Maryland. He was a little bit confused at the total insanity of this holiday game, but he did everything he could to help decipher the clues. Then there was me, a communications expert, entrepreneur and artist...definitely a creative type. The kids, Michael and Matt, did their part by cheering us on! As entrepreneur and administrator, we spent a lot of time interpreting the clue but little time in planning our route. We made sure we were headed in the right direction, but we didn't put a lot of thought as to the most efficient way to get there. We were too busy thinking about our ultimate goal: the treasure! If we were an organization, it could be said we spent our time forming our mission and vision, but we lacked an efficient, thought-out execution plan and that led to our failure.

The Tacticians: Julie's Team

In my sister Julie's car was my husband Rich, who grew up one town over and was an engineer; my sister Julie, who was the chief financial officer for large construction company at that time; my brother-in-law Mark, who grew up in Pennsylvania and was a banker; and my nieces Liz and Courtney who were seven and six. Most of the clues were in places that had a variety of routes to get there. The engineer, the CFO and the banker had a very systematic approach to planning out the best and fastest way to the next destination. They took a look at their clues then analyzed the traffic pattern to deduce the shortest route available. Before they put their Suburban into gear, they created their plan and execution tactics and then engaged in the hunt...leading to victory!

The Peacemakers: Sheila's Team

In my sister Sheila's car was my brother's wife Laura, a stay-at-home mom who graduated from Cal Berkley with a degree in social work; my sister Sheila, who was a business teacher; and Kevin, Shawny Boy and Nicole, ages eight, seven and three. Although they got off to a quick start, this team found that when leadership (Sheila and Laura) is managed by the collaboration of all team members ("What kind of ice cream do you want? And you? And you?") they lost precious time that was critical to the outcome of their project (finding the treasure). They were still eating ice cream in a booth at Friendly's while all three other teams had completed the hunt, leaving them in a dismal last place. But at least the ice cream made everyone on the team happy!

The "Funsters": Pete and Kate's Team

In an unusual move, Mimi teamed my brother Pete and sister Kate together to head a team. Because of the wide age difference between Kate and I (nine years) it was difficult to write clues that would be known to both of us since we essentially grew up in different time periods. To even things up, Mimi partnered Kate with Peter who would remember much more about our collective childhood than she would. So Pete and Kate were co-captains. My brother Peter is a serial entrepreneur, with a background in sales. He is all about relationships and having fun. Since his move to California with his family, this has only deepened. Kate is an assistant recreation director, majoring in the area of "play" in college! I was pretty convinced at the start of the hunt this would be the winning team. My mother must have felt this way, too, because she gave Peter a slight handicap: strapped to his chest was his baby daughter Hannah. Also on his team were his three year-old son Tom and our eleven-year old nephew Jason. With all of these young children, I think that a case of the "sillies" to keep their large group of kids entertained and having fun cost Kate and Pete the hunt.

Motivating a grumbling crowd of teenagers or keeping a mob of tiny tots interested in a game can be a supremely tough task, but Mimi was always up for the challenge. She remains a mixture of Mary Poppins and Carol Brady. She brought a playful and positive environment to every aspect of our childhood and does so even now in our adulthood. Mimi is still described today by my father as the family "funster." With five kids, she did a lot of playing as a young mother, and now in her retirement, she still enjoys the company of playmates because of the close relationships she has developed with her four daughters, her son, their spouses and all of her wonderful grandchildren. And from her, we've all learned how to add an element of fun to everything in our lives, especially those difficult tasks that require a little hard work. With Mimi as a guide, we can turn even the most mundane of life's activities into a game!

Simple Truth from Mom:
Life is a game...don't forget to play!

Having a job that you find joyful is a blessing beyond belief. Understanding how to find that joy in a challenging work environment is a different story. The ability to blend productivity with a positive environment is a skill that has a large payoff for a manager and a mom. By taking Mimi's lessons and applying them in the workplace, I've found that I have been able to challenge my team to work harder but do it in a way that's joyful.

Many times we inherit teams that need some life pumped into them. Mimi had this same challenge each year when she had new students in her classroom. She took her approach at home and applied it at work in the classroom.

I know this playful purpose is as applicable in the business world as it was in our home and in Mimi's nursery school classroom. I've seen many corporate activities that have taken a page from Mimi's fun and positive approach produce amazing results in productivity for the workplace.

WHOSE TEAM AM I ON?

About seven years ago, I was called in to work with a large company that was consolidating two of their divisions into a single department. My team was selected to coach everyone through this transitional process because we had previously worked with members from each of the original groups, and we understood the history between them.

Due to the structure of the organization, the two divisions were essentially competitors, both vying for project work. One group was comprised of contractors hired as outsourced employees who mainly focused on short-range projects. The other group were direct employees of the company, and their focus was primarily long-term projects. However, when projects were scarce and jobs were on the line, these two groups were forced to play tug-of-war with each other over every project, creating tension between them.

Eventually, the corporation decided having these two separate groups of essentially the same skill sets was redundant, and they were determined to pull the two groups together into a single team. This sudden shift resulted in an uneasy and strained relationship between these new team members and how they were going to work together. The newly appointed director of the organization found himself with the monumental task of bringing this team together and building trust among them while maintaining high productivity in the process.

As a trusted advisor to this director, my team and I were brought in to create an off-site team building experience to start these professional project managers moving forward as a cohesive team. This was quite a challenge because of the lack of cooperation and general mistrust between these two groups. Working in conjunction with this director — and remembering Mimi's mantra of "Life's a game to play," — we created an off-site program that combined a playful atmosphere where the team could relax and laugh together with exercises to build mutual respect and ensure the team could work together to accomplish their project tasks. The goal of our off-site program was to lay a foundation that would become a launching point for this team to learn to work cohesively. I decided to accomplish this objective in a way that pushed everyone out of their comfort zone, forcing them into non-work-related scenarios where winning depended on everyone participating and engaging completely. So we brought this urban group of professionals into the middle of the woods to stay in cabins for three days!

TEAM BUILDING IN THE WOODS

Our repertoire of activities was vast: we combined traditional business development activities with unconventional exercises. On the first day, we had the team develop a timeline that showed the evolution of their department, a team-skills analysis to help everyone understand the talents of each team member, and a SWOT (Strengths, Weaknesses, Opportunities and Threats) analysis to take a snapshot of where the team was at that point in time. We engaged the team in discussions about the new organizational structure and their project assignments. Our goal for the day was to get the team to understand the charter of their new group and how work would be assigned among them in the future. These activities provided a solid base for Day Two.

On the second day, with the attendees getting more comfortable in their tree-filled surroundings, I helped them stretch and learn to play together. Remembering Mimi's treasure hunt and they way that she organized her children, I broke the attendees into teams that mirrored their new work groups and sent them into the woods on a scavenger hunt I developed from information I gathered at the pre-offsite interviews I had conducted. I drafted clues and questions based on each individual's work experience, projects, educational background, and even their hobbies. The teams competed to see who would win the honor of getting out of doing clean-up and chores for the remainder of the two days in the woods. The second place team had to cook dinner that night for the other teams, and the poor team who came in last had to do all the cleaning! Since each team was a mix of people from both of the old departments, new alliances were formed between these former competitors. And they were certainly motivated to work together! All of the teams raced around the grounds looking for clues and laughing together, and after the winning team was crowned, there was a new atmosphere of friendly teasing and joking among the group, even as requests for food were dished out by the winners!

TIME TO GET REAL

After the lighthearted scavenger hunt, the new team was ready to begin working together on a real challenge that would test their newfound alliances. In homage to my ROTC Captain — Captain Empowerment — I took the teams out to the Ropes course, a series of obstacle-type stations created with ropes and walls. At each post, the team had to all pull together to get every last member through the obstacle course in spite of everyone's differences in size and athletic ability. I watched as these former competitors rallied together to hoist each other over walls, balance on tight ropes strung between trees, and swing over the stream. They never left anyone behind or let anyone give up; soon all three teams became one. And all the while one of my staff members was taking pictures to document this newfound camaraderie.

That night the director and I decided it was time to address some of the team's real issues. Playing together would only solve some of their differences, and we both knew there were years of competition to overcome. After dinner, we walked the group out to the lake and together we built a bonfire. We all sat in Adirondack chairs around the fire, and I began to ask questions that led the group through some difficult conversations. The atmosphere of fun created by our exercises opened a door that allowed the group to speak more freely with each other and to lay to rest the fears they faced in having to work together.

MISSION ACCOMPLISHED

On the last morning as we were eating breakfast, I noticed a canoe out on the lake with two people fishing. When I looked to see who was missing from our group, I couldn't believe it! The men who were fishing together had been the fiercest competitors within the two groups! They never seemed to have a nice word to say about each other. Frankly, they were the two who the director and I feared would never become true teammates. And there they were, fishing together!

While on the scavenger hunt working on the same team, they discovered they were both fishing nuts, and they had each brought their poles along to the retreat. As they searched for the next clues, they shared techniques and tips with each other. Later on, at the campfire, they decided to get up two hours earlier than the rest of the group, swipe the canoe from behind the main cabin, and steal some fishing time before breakfast. They came in about an hour late to the morning session, hungry and smelling of fish while boasting of each other's catches that morning. As I surveyed these two opposites interacting as teammates and friends, I said to myself, "Mission accomplished!"

Lipstick Leadership

"My mother, Joyce Mullet Ross, had one particular gift that eclipsed all of her other mothering skills. She allowed me to be whoever I wanted to be. She encouraged it, in

fact. She didn't have any preconceived ideas about what I should do or what I should 'be' when I grew up. If I wanted to play the piano, she found me a teacher. If I wanted to play sports and be in the play, she didn't make me choose one or the other. She let my own desire and intuition guide me to make the choices that were best for me. She gave me the space to discover who I am, and as I continue to build my own business I am continually grateful for my mother. She allowed me a wide space in which to create my life. This gave me confidence and a wonderful sense of independence. I honor my mother's lesson by allowing those who work for me to do the job that best suits their talents and personality. I remember to always give them space to shine."

~ Dr. Patricia A. Ross, www.BestAffirmations.com

**Submit your best "Mom's Wisdom" story at
www.LipstickLeadership.com today!**

The relationship between playtime and productivity is powerful. Because we were able to help the team relax through play, they were also able to work through most of their issues. They were now able to communicate in a trusting environment, and that was greatly increased with their now positive attitudes regarding their new situation. That trust was nurtured and cultivated throughout the rest of the year, improving the cohesiveness of the group along the way. My team created large displays of the photographs we took over those three days, and posted them at the entrance to their building. The collage included funny pictures of each other so they were reminded of their ability to laugh and play together, keeping that spirit of joy in their daily work.

So as a manager or a member of a team, remember Mimi's lesson: don't forget to play!!!

MBA (Mom's Business Acumen) Class: It Pays to Play! Getting More from Your Team

To get your team to play together as a way to improve working conditions, you need to do research on your team. Create a folder of information about every member and use that information to build an offsite experience or run a special project that gives back to the community in some way while simultaneously developing more cohesion within your team. You'll be amazed at how the team blossoms when work is taken out of the picture for a short amount of time!

Here are some of things you can find out about your team to find the kind of activities to build a playful environment and bond that they can then apply to their work:

a. What do your team members like to do during off hours? Cooking, hiking, boating, golfing, reading — all important information!

b. If they have children, how old are they?

c. Where did they go to school or grow up?

d. Where have they worked in the past?

e.   What are they afraid of?

f.   What would they change about their live or themselves?

g.   What aspect of their job do they like best and least?

h.   If money was no object, what would they do with their lives?

i.   What charitable organizations are they involved in?

The more you understand your team, the better you'll be able to choose the type of activities that they'll all enjoy. And when they're having fun, they'll be building stronger bonds than could ever be achieved sitting through a stuffy lecture on teamwork! The alliances and friendships formed during these activities will be carried over into the workplace, and you'll find that because they're comfortable with each other, they'll be a more cohesive — and productive — team at work, too!

So don't wait or make excuses: do your research, make a plan and set a "play-date" today for your team, and you'll be amazed with the results that a happy, unified team can produce!

CHAPTER 3

STAY OUT OF THE KITCHEN

MEALS WITH THE YOZZOS

My Aunt Marie was my father's younger sister by seven years, and his only sibling. She was tall, graceful and a classic beauty, which was unusual in our family of short, expressive (read: *loud*), and earthy Italians. As the only girl in an Italian immigrant family, a large amount of the housework fell to my aunt. My grandmother, Nana, was a seamstress in New York City and worked long hours to support the family, leaving much of the caring for the men to Maria.

While it was a small family by Italian standards, the extended family was very large. "The family" here in America included cousins, second cousins, aunts, uncles, grandparents, and any other immigrant relatives who came over on the boat and needed a home-cooked meal after their long journey. This huge extended family was a part of everyday life — especially at mealtime. Today, we would call what they did every night "entertaining company," but for them it was just life in an Italian household. Each evening, the entire family congregated in large groups, ate huge quantities of food and drank massive amounts of my grandfather's homemade dandelion wine. This made for quite a boisterous and down-to-earth environment for my Aunt Marie to grow up in.

HOLIDAYS — ITALIAN STYLE

When Aunt Marie married Uncle Bill, they moved to Connecticut. About the same time, my father and my mother, Mimi, moved out to Long Island. Now they were about an hour and a half from New York City and the tight knit Italian community they grew up in. Each had children: Aunt Marie had my four cousins — Bill, Kathy, Patty and Tom — and my parents had me and my four siblings. Even though the two families lived two hours apart, we continued the tradition of making sure the holidays were spent with the entire extended family. Holidays meant getting together — usually as early as the beginning of the holiday week — to enjoy the festivities culminating in a huge feast with my cousins, aunts, uncles, grandparents, second cousins and usually a couple of stragglers from the neighborhood. Every year, these celebrations would be held at a different house, either my grandmother's, my mother's, or my Aunt Marie's. Soon the family grew too large for my grandmother's house, and my mother and Aunt Marie alternated homes hosting these holiday meals.

These were no ordinary meals: the holiday meal was always six or seven courses! The eating began midday and went well into the night. It was a major production that required cooking for weeks before to make the homemade sauces, soups, pastas, bread and desserts. And that didn't even include the actual main course! The orchestration of the meal, getting everything cooked and out on the table at the right time and temperature — while trying to control a mob of over thirty people — was complicated to say the least.

Lipstick Leadership

"My grandmother was one of the friendliest people you've ever seen. She was curious about others and took an interest in everyone she met. She was well-liked by everyone she came across. She'd be in a long line for the ladies room when we'd go to the ballet, and she'd make a new best friend with the woman in line next to her, sharing some little treat from her 'pocket-book.' She also treated everyone the same whether it

was a nurse changing a bedpan or the daughter-in-law of the owner of the Super Bowl Champions. In business, I've found that kindness, curiosity and just plain being nice go a long way. Taking a genuine interest in the hardworking secretary is as important as being friendly to the boss. Sharing — whether it is a free giveaway that you bring back from a convention for that hard-working secretary or a helpful piece of information for a colleague — is just a good way to go through life. Some people may think it's not 'business-like' to act in that way, but actually, it goes a long way and is just plain good business to be well-liked."

~ Marla Libraty, www.ExtendFertility.com

Advance your career with the help of Michelle's FREE e-zine. Sign up today at www.LipstickLeadership.com!

Both Aunt Marie and Mimi had their own style in how they executed the holiday meal in their home. However, there was one unbreakable rule of the holiday meal: the hostess was in charge. Mom was the leader in her own kitchen as was Aunt Marie in hers. Being able to adjust in each other's habits, style and expectations in the kitchen was a pretty monumental task for these strong women leaders. To the credit of both my mother and my aunt, I never remember a moment of tension or an angry word as they executed this "business critical" task (the holiday meal) for their "organization" (our extended family). When Aunt Marie was in my mother's kitchen, she completely deferred to the instructions of my mother, and my mother reciprocated when she was in Aunt Marie's kitchen. This was a wonderful lesson in leadership and teamwork for us to see as children, grandchildren, and as women. This important dynamic showed us you can be strong, assertive, know your mind and what you want, and yet still be able to follow someone else's lead and respect their approach even though it might be very different from your own.

THE COOKING HISTORY OF MIMI AND MARIE

My mother's approach to the holiday meals was one she learned as an adult. She grew up in a wealthy, cultured household with a mother, Mops, who was uncomfortable and awkward in the kitchen. Mops was accustomed to having a kitchen staff that prepared all of the meals. When my mother married my father and was initiated into his Italian household and traditions, she watched my father's family in the kitchen, always questioning, researching and helping Aunt Marie, Nana and my Great Aunt Jennie to be able to learn how to prepare the holiday meals. She wanted to be able to recreate those traditions for my father and her children because she knew how much they meant to my father and how much they would mean to us growing up. In this, Mimi taught me an important message about family: when you love and care about someone, sometimes it means you have to stretch yourself and learn new things to make them happy. In the early days of my mother's cooking, my father would stop at the pizzeria on his way home because he wasn't sure if what she was testing out in the kitchen would be edible! I remember my mom as the amazing cook she is today and always was for me growing up, but it was a skill she learned as a young woman because she was motivated to bring a better quality of "product" to her new "organization."

My Aunt Marie, on the other hand, was surrounded by amazing cooks growing up. She was familiar with the kitchen and the market, and she knew exactly what ingredients she needed to take every dish to perfection. Aunt Marie was very, very particular about every item that went into the food she prepared. She would go to the market the week before her turn to host a holiday and examine every piece of fruit, meat, cheese, and herb before an item made its way into her shopping cart. Everything had to be of the highest quality; there was no room for compromise. Aunt Marie took tremendous pride in how she put together her table. Her full-time job was being a housewife and a mother, and she did this with the kind of gusto, enthusiasm and incredible attention to detail that would rival any CEO as she expertly juggled the tasks entailed in running her "organization."

AUNT MARIE'S FEASTS

When we were young, and it was Aunt Marie's turn to host the festivities, the holidays meant arriving a few days before the actual event and staying a few days after. But as we became teenagers and had athletic commitments, we began to arrive the morning of the holiday. After we went to Mass as a family, my parents would bundle all five of us into the car to make the two-hour drive to Aunt Marie's.

Lipstick Leadership

"When girlfriends bond, they create the sound of music. When they bond together for a common cause, they create a symphony of unlimited and immeasurable orchestral power."

~ Heshie Segal, The JetNetting Connection

Submit your best "Mom's Wisdom" story at www.LipstickLeadership.com today!

The thing I remember most about those holidays is the assault on our senses the moment we opened the back door to Aunt Marie's home. We would be bombarded with the most amazing smells, and those smells would light a fire under our feet! We would rush toward them, hoping for a taste of heavenly food, only to run into Aunt Marie standing at the entrance to her kitchen with her hand held up. We would skid to a halt as she said, "STOP! Don't come into the kitchen!" After a big, warm embrace from her, Aunt Marie would order us into the other room while she finished preparations in the kitchen. She knew she needed to be able to concentrate on her strategic plan for the meal in order to get all of the courses out and presented in a way that was pleasing to the eye as well as the palate. She needed to be organized and uninterrupted — even with nine children, her husband, her brother and sister-in-law, parents, cousins and a few stragglers all racing around her home.

Many hands were eager to help…and sneak a morsel off a platter here or there, too (after all, we were just human and it smelled so wonderful!) but Aunt Marie would not allow us in the kitchen right away. We would have to hover in her great room where we were tortured by the sumptuous smells until she invited us in.

This was how Aunt Marie worked in her domain. She needed those moments of quiet in the kitchen to get herself and the meal completely organized before the chaos of the family bombarded her. And when she was ready, she would call from the kitchen and invite us one-by-one inside where she would delegate a task to each of us. My mother was always the first guest in the kitchen to assist with the cooking. As the oldest grandchild, I was usually the next one in and asked to do things like check the table setting or cut vegetables. Aunt Marie was always very clear about exactly how she wanted every task executed because she had the overall vision of what the outcome was supposed to look, taste and feel like.

At the end of each meal, the family was happy, content and full. We had all pitched in, each in different ways thanks to Aunt Marie's knowledge of our skills. Some of us cleared away dirty dishes; some of us cooked; some of us set up furniture and decorated, and some of us watched the little children so others could complete different tasks. But at the end of each meal, we knew we had come together and had put out an experience each one of us would cherish — an outcome in which we could be proud of our own individual contribution.

KITCHEN LEADERSHIP IN THE BOARDROOM

Aunt Marie knew what the table would look like and what response she would get from us as we tasted, smelled and saw the food, so she would know success or failure by comparing her vision of success with the reality of our reaction. But to make that vision a reality she had to be able to understand all the moving parts of preparing the perfect meal and then communicate directly the actions she wanted us to take to support her desired outcome.

If my mother had come into Aunt Marie's kitchen and pushed her ideas of how things should be seasoned, cooked, or presented, there would have been friction and tension surrounding the holidays. It would have also clouded the ultimate goal and created confusion and chaos — and probably a lot of burned dishes! In order for the meal to be a success, Aunt Marie had to paint a clear picture of her vision and then completely engage my mother in achieving that outcome. My mother was confident enough that when her turn came to lead at the next holiday in her home, Aunt Marie would follow her. The relationship of these two very strong and very different women is not only a touching story of family, but it is a powerful story of how two women leaders in an organization can co-exist and help each other shine. The leadership qualities of Aunt Marie and my mother were not diminished by the success of each others' meals, and ultimately, the "organization" of my family clearly benefited from their triumphs in the kitchen!

Lipstick Leadership

"My mom taught me how important it is to have girl-friends to support you. She did this socially, but I do this where I work. I seek out older women or women with more experience than me to be my friends and part of my work support system. I do the same for the younger women with less experience in my industry, providing them with support."

~ Martha Con Hultzman, CPA; Lefkowiz, Garfinkel, Champi & DeRienzo P.C.

Advance your career with the help of Michelle's FREE e-zine. Sign up today at www.LipstickLeadership.com!

The skills learned in Aunt Marie's kitchen have been skills I draw from on a daily basis at work. I execute projects the same way as she did, whether the project is cooking for the holidays in my home or executing a nationwide commercial marketing campaign for a corporate client. I make sure I have a clear vision of the outcome so I know what success looks like.

My Aunt Marie passed away last year after a long battle with cancer, but who she is and what she has taught me and my family will always be with us. That is the true gift of leadership: even when the leader is not right there guiding you, you can still draw upon their teachings and apply them in your life.

Simple Truth from Mom:
Know how to lead and how to follow.

The lesson of knowing when to lead and how to follow is an important one. It is not a weakness to follow; it's only a weakness if you have been given the opportunity to lead and you don't step up and take advantage of it. As women, we need to be prepared to lead and to always be looking for leadership opportunities; however, we also need to be able to lead in a way that does not step on someone else's project in the process.

The Yozzo family "team" was accepting of both Mimi and Aunt Marie as leaders, and having faith that your team is going to follow you is crucial to your success as a leader.

THE APPRENTICE

I host a weekly radio talk show called "Workplace Wisdom." My show focuses on bringing new business and career-related ideas to my listeners to arm them with everything they need for success at work. The show has brought me the opportunity to interview very interesting people, including some of the leading management minds of our time.

I was particularly impressed by a young man, Sean Yazbeck, who I interviewed after he was a contestant on Donald Trump's reality show *The Apprentice* airing on NBC. Not only did Sean participate in the fifth season of *The Apprentice*, he won the coveted job with Trump's organization!

The premise of *The Apprentice* is basically this: it is a televised job interview process, pitting candidates against each other in a highly competitive environment while forcing them to not only work together as teams but also live together, isolated from their friends and families! Each week, the teams are tasked with a project and evaluated on their individual performance, their teams' performance, and the task's level of completion and success. Every task brings a new team leader — or project manager as they're called — creating a rotating system of leadership within the teams. So last week's team leader suddenly finds him or herself in the position of having to follow someone else this week — you can imagine the flared tempers and chaos that sometimes erupts during these challenges! The losing team then has to go the board room and face Donald Trump as they try to defend themselves. Ultimately, the blame of their team failure is placed on someone and that person is fired.

VYING TO BE THE NEXT *APPRENTICE*

Job hunting in general is an emotional and stressful experience, but putting it all out there in front of millions of people brings it to a completely different level. Sean shared with me his thoughts on what it takes to lead and follow successfully.

The candidate pool contained people who ranged in age from 22 to 38. They came from different countries and cultures, and were raised in very different economic situations. Diversity and incongruent approaches to leadership became an issue right off the bat. Many of the candidates boasted degrees from the top universities in the country — Harvard, Columbia, Northwestern and Cornell University, to just name a few — and each held high-level professional jobs as doctors, lawyers, fundraisers, and entrepreneurs. This was a talented and highly skilled bunch of people. Ego always enters the picture when you collect a group of high performers who are accustomed to running the show. And according to Sean, the task of following seemed to be harder than the task of leading for some of the candidates.

Sean and I agreed: as a leader, you must believe in yourself as well as believe in your team. Having true confidence in your convictions is essential. You must have faith that if you put your mind to it, you can achieve anything. A leader who can project that kind of confidence will not have difficulty finding a team willing to follow. If at the same time that leader validates the team members by seeking their input and council on project execution, they will have more power to get the job done efficiently.

SEAN'S APPROACH TO LEADERSHIP

In *Winning*, by Jack Welch, he wrote, "Before you become a leader, success is all about growing yourself. When you become a leader, success is all about growing others." Sean held onto these words of wisdom as he competed as a leader and as a team member following others during his time on *The Apprentice*. I asked him to describe why his leadership style succeeded in getting him the job as Trump's *Apprentice*:

This is what he told me:

> "I surround myself with a team consisting of individuals that embody integrity, intelligence, maturity, and passion. I believe far more can be achieved by a leader who allows individuals to feel empowered, valued, and motivated than a leader who micromanages every moving part of a task. So I evaluate, coach, and build self-confidence within my team, and only intervene in their individual task implementation when necessary. This approached kept my team engaged while I was leading and positioned me as a trusted team member when I was following.
>
> "A positive leader with a positive outlook will end up managing a positive team. And when a team of talented individuals works well together, they'll win every time. It's near impossible to get along with everyone all of the time, but to meet your goals, you must concentrate on managing relationships with your team, your customer and

your management, and a crucial part of that is knowing how to lead and follow."

My interview with Sean was a delightful exploration of leadership under pressure from a man who clearly understands the value of others. Just like Mimi and Aunt Marie, Sean knows how to "stay out of the kitchen" and how to step up as a leader. Lead on Sean!

MBA (Mom's Business Acumen) Class: Tips for Powerful Leadership

Pitching ideas to a strong leader can be challenging, but by realizing the power of your idea, you'll gain the confidence to step up and lead a group of leaders!

Here are some tips to help you jump from follower to leader with a few simple adjustments:

1. Always know the impact of your idea on your organization — results always get noticed, and if you can prove them statistically, even better!

2. Match the confidence level of the leader when presenting your concept to the group. They're accustomed to following the leader's style, and they won't question your ability to lead a new initiative if they're familiar with how you communicate with them.

3. Be succinct and to the point in your delivery. Powerful leaders are seldom long-winded, and they never beat around the bush!

4. Understand what's in it for each of your listeners to back your idea. A clear path to how they might bene-

fit from the positive outcome of your project will help you rally support.

5. Know what the objections might be raised even before you launch into your plan. Address them before they're voiced by acknowledging the issue and describing how you researched and solved the obstacle.

6. Flash that smile, but don't giggle! I've seen many professional women dissolve into nervous giggles during the Q&A section of a presentation. DON'T! It gives away your power, and you'll need it, sister!

7. Believe the response will be positive and proceed with that knowledge. You'll be amazed at how that belief projects the end result you desire!

There is nothing more rewarding than leading a team to success. So the next time your team is assembled, keep a look out for the opportunity to lead. And if it doesn't happen today, then be sure to engage as a team member and follow the leader. The key to great success is to contribute!

Tap into my GOLDEN ROLODEX of experts that I've collected from my years as a radio talk show host and corporate coach. Get a taste of what my expert friends can share with you to help propel your career by joining me at CEOSecretBlueprint.com.

For a LIMITED TIME I'm offering an e-course program scholarship to my readers. To join me for FREE, just enter K2CO as your code to waive the $279 cost of this e-course. I guarantee this program will change the way you think and work and will lead you to a more prosperous and fulfilling career (and that means more money!)

CHAPTER 4

TOOTHPASTE AND TOWELS

MORNINGS WITH MIMI

As every mother knows, the morning is a stressful time of day. It is a time when everyone in the house has to move in a rhythm that gets them all cleaned, fed, and out the door. One misstep and your day can start on a sour note that will affect everything that comes after it, all day long. As a mom, we want everyone — including ourselves — to start the day in a positive fashion — you know, *rise and shine!*

Lipstick Leadership

"What I've learned from my four kids — and from the experiences of moms I've interviewed for my book — is the importance of consistency in children's' lives. This is especially true when it comes to a mom's job. Whether a mom works part-time or full-time or has been home since her children were born, it's the predictability of the arrangement that makes it work for the kids. Messing with that consistency can be tricky — which is why moving in and out of the workforce must be handled with great care."

~ Carol Fishman Cohen, Co-Author of "Back on the Career Track"

Submit your best "Mom's Wisdom" story at www.LipstickLeadership.com today!

Growing up in my mother Mimi's house, our morning ritual actually started *the night before*. It began with my mother trying to determine who had the greatest need for the bathroom the next morning. With four sisters, my poor brother Peter didn't have a prayer of getting a shower in the morning, so he usually showered at night. (On that same "female domination of the bathroom" note, I was convinced my father never needed to shower at all — I never heard the shower going when he was in the bathroom in all my years growing up because he always opted to shower in the middle of the night after we all were fast asleep!) So Mimi would assess which of us girls needed to wash her hair in the morning so it would be easier to style. If you just needed a shower and no hair washing, you drew an evening shower and had to deal with bed-head, leaving less chaos in bathroom the next morning.

Since our bathroom was considered community space, my father thought of ingenious ways to fix it so more than one person could use it at the same time. He installed double sinks and attached a full-length mirror to the wall over the sinks sideways so all of us teenage girls could get ready at different stages while sharing the only bathroom with a shower.

A typical morning with Mimi overseeing our assembly line style of bathroom management would begin with my sister Julie rising first and heading into the shower. After Julie finished in the shower and dried off, she remained in the bathroom. I usually came in next, and I jumped into the shower while Julie stood at the first sink — the one with the electrical outlet — to dry her hair. My sister Sheila had the toughest time getting up in the morning so she usually brought up the rear (my youngest sister Kate went to a school that started an hour after the rest of us left, so she was lucky enough not to have to share the bathroom in the morning at all!). As Sheila started her shower, Julie would move to the second sink to brush her teeth and put on any makeup, and I would start drying my hair. We all would shift positions until we had shared the bathroom efficiently and had all finished getting ready.

Sometimes we would hear banging at the door as Peter tried to enter, but he never made it past the hallway! Thanks to Mimi's system, we managed to avoid fighting over mirrors, collisions in the shower, and eyes poked by mascara brushes...most of the time!

NEARBY TOWN...WORLDS APART

In the next town over, there was an even busier household moving through their morning ritual. At my mother-in-law, Marty Drake's house, there were twelve children — six boys and six girls — and a husband to get out the door every morning. It was nothing short of a miracle that they were all clean, clothed, fed, and on time. Picture this: twelve children under the age of sixteen and a husband vying for bathroom time in one bathroom. Add to it six dogs, two horses, five loaves of bread and four dozen eggs to make French toast, three gallons of milk, oh, and throw in a couple of paper routes, and you have a typical morning for Marty Drake. And with such a brood to handle, there was no room for discussion when it came to Marty's house rules. The rules were not broken because the consequences — from not only Marty, but from the mob of siblings as well — were swift and severe.

Lipstick Leadership

"My sister and I were really into Rice Krispies Treats. Mom decided to make some for company that would arrive later in the afternoon. My mom hated to read recipes when she could just figure how to make a dish on her own. Well, the treats Mom made that day were less than successful so she decided to add more ingredients and turn her concoction into a cake. That wasn't quite right either, so she added some more stuff and made these really thin, strange looking cookies that were FANTASTIC! Our company arrived and was so impressed that they wanted the recipe, which my sister and I thought was very funny! In business you can create some predictability when you follow the recipe, but you can also miss out on intuitive genius. My mom always made fun interesting, unique and wonderful dishes because she allowed her creativity to guide her; as an entrepreneur...I try to do the same thing!"

~ Elaine Starling, www.PromisePower.com

**Advance your career with the help of
Michelle's FREE e-zine. Sign up today at
www.LipstickLeadership.com!**

With one functioning bathroom and fourteen people in the house, everyone getting a hot shower in the morning was out of the question. The coveted bathroom was at the bottom of the back staircase of the family's large Dutch Colonial home. To get to the bathroom, you had to go upstairs to the bedrooms and down the back staircase, ending at the bathroom door. This meant there was a lot of teenage traffic up and down that staircase in the morning! Marty had the younger children shower the night before, but that hardly put a dent in the activity left for the morning. While Marty cooked at her restaurant-style stove, her kids followed the system she devised and scrambled to get time in the bathroom.

Since in the Drake house, time in the bathroom was the only place anyone was guaranteed a few moments to themselves, securing a few precious moments in the bathroom was top priority. Before Marty developed her system, it was a madhouse of a line of kids waiting on the stairs to keep their place. This led to plenty of arguments and shouting matches, and because the kids stood there waiting, some of them ended up missing breakfast. Over time — and after a few frustrating and hungry mornings for some of the kids — Marty came up with an adjustment to this system.

Her new system required two things to happen: first, after you woke up, you needed to grab your towel, toothpaste and toiletries and put them on the closest unclaimed step outside the bathroom. The luckiest person was the first one in line: he or she usually got both a hot shower *and* a hot breakfast! If you didn't wake up early and act fast enough, you were assured the last place in line and a shocking cold shower! Second, after you captured a step, you needed to weigh your hunger with your need for a warm shower because to actually get into the bathroom, you had to be present on the step when the bathroom door opened; otherwise, the person on the step behind you claimed the bathroom sanctuary as theirs. On any given morning, you could look down those stairs and on each one would be a towel and toiletries while the kids used their waiting time to dress, have breakfast or do a little last minute homework.

All morning long, the Drake kids would run up the back staircase and then down the front stairs to the kitchen to grab their portion of the buffet-style breakfast stacked on the kitchen island, and then they'd run the opposite way to make sure they were on their stair when the bathroom door opened. The speed with which you could eat breakfast was a distinct advantage because the faster you ate, the better chance you had at keeping your place in line — and it also helped to protect your food from hungry siblings looking for more! "Breakfast and a shower" was certainly a balancing act in the Drake household!

Lipstick Leadership

"My grandmother had a few choice sayings that nearly half a century later still ring true. One of her favorites was 'The sooner you get done, you'll be done.' This is particularly true of boring, difficult or unappealing projects. If you can think about how much better you'll feel

after you have them out of the way, it makes it a lot easier to jump in and take charge."

~ Linda J. Popky, President, L2M Associates

**Submit your best "Mom's Wisdom" story at
www.LipstickLeadership.com today!**

THE STRATEGY OF A HOT BREAKFAST AND A HOT SHOWER

My husband Rich was strategic on how he worked this system. He observed the length of time each person habitually spent in the bathroom; for instance, if he knew he was following a sister, he had a little more time to eat. He also took note of who might linger longer for a second helping at the breakfast table — his athletic brothers were often a hungry bunch of guys! And there was always the possibility he could jump a turn if he was poised on his step with no one in front of him when the bathroom door opened. Rich's observations began to increase his odds of actually getting a hot meal *and* a hot shower. The only glitch would be if his father was running late — he trumped anyone on any step at any time!

While this system may have seemed to involve quite a bit of movement and a little bit of chance, the alternative was fist-fights and yelling matches that inevitably would break out without any system at all. In a household where discipline ruled, the prospect of letting the teenagers run loose every morning to *figure it out* on their own was unacceptable. An organized system was the only logical solution to keeping chaos at bay, and Marty's simple system of toothpaste and towels worked like a charm!

Simple Truth from Mom:
Even the simplest of systems can create
order out of chaos

When you are in the middle of a chaotic situation, sometimes it is difficult to see a clear path to order. Taking the time to understand the overall climate and the players involved in your situation can help you develop a system that will keep the team all working toward a common goal in an orderly fashion. The different approaches Mimi and Marty took to solve the same problem were a direct result of their individual style of leadership, the level of "morning madness" in each home, the architectural limitations, and the complexity and size of the each family. A good leader has the skills to analyze each element of a system to ensure the successful outcome of implementation — just like Mimi and Marty did.

THE COST-SAVING CONUNDRUM

My consulting team was recently hired to work with the site management team for a large multi-million dollar corporation whose new CEO challenged them to get the best pricing and quality deals they could command. The site management team consisted of directors from several company departments: facility management, employee health and safety, project engineering, creative services, and operational service departments. Each department director was asked to reduce their expense budget by 20%. Before we were hired, management hastily rolled out an aggressive cost-savings initiative to their employees, and they were greeted with grumbling up and down the

Lipstick Leadership

"My daughters taught me how may activities I could cram into one day! A sign in my office states: 'I thought there were only 24 hours in a day until I went into business for myself,' but the truth is that having one's own business AND raising children is what really teaches that lesson."

~ Wendy Lazar, Glendale/ ParadeStore.com

Advance your career with the help of Michelle's FREE e-zine. Sign up today at www.LipstickLeadership.com!

line. The staff claimed there was no place else to draw savings from without layoffs, and there was too much work to lose manpower. This posed quite a challenge for the management team. Enter my consulting team.

Barbara was the director of the project engineering group which was responsible for the planning and execution of major construction and renovation of all the corporation's existing facilities. Building complex manufacturing plants for the company required a large number of vendors, each providing a multitude of services: architects, space planners, painters, process specialists, builders, HVAC systems specialists, and overall project managers.

Traditionally, Barbara's department outsourced some of the construction project management services their workload required. They procured these services from a large number of vendors — from independent consultants to large multinational firms. With upwards of 70 different projects per year to manage, keeping track of the cost and quality for each vendor and all the different categories of services was quite a challenge for Barbara's group!

OUT WITH THE OLD

In an effort to contribute to cost-cutting goals, Barbara enlisted my team to begin the development of a new vendor management system that would help her senior team analyze where they could cut costs without sacrificing quality. In the same way Marty fixed the inefficiency of the morning household chaos with her unique system, Barbara was ready to tackle the messy vendor management process and turn it into her own efficient "toothpaste and towels" system.

In the past, as a specific need arose in the department, the group added new personnel via "word-of-mouth" recommendations. A project manager in the company would recommend a colleague with the skills set required for the job, and that individual would be contacted about the possibility of coming on board as a contract employee. This random "system" produced both amazing and awful results. Too many managers were more concerned about helping

Lipstick Leadership

"My first boss (a woman) shared a tip with me that has made a huge impact on my life and business: Take a notebook and pen with you everywhere and take notes during your conversations. Ideas may spring up later when you review your notes...and it ensures you won't forget anything! Now I am a compulsive note taker and my clients value my creativity and project management skills—all created via my notes!"

~ Elaine Starling, www.PromisePower.com

Submit your best "Mom's Wisdom" story at
www.LipstickLeadership.com today!

their buddies get work than with quality and cost savings. More than a few contractors were hired even though their skills were not exemplary and their prices were through the roof.

The number of vendors contracting with the company had quickly ballooned and was completely out of control. Did the company really need over two dozen vendors specializing in painting? The enormous vendor group made it nearly impossible to keep track of each one efficiently.

With so many different vendors, there was also a vast array of differing project management methodologies, resulting in scheduling nightmares. Tasks were being done out of order, resulting in messes and miscommunications that made prices skyrocket. An inconsistent fee structure among vendors often led to confusion and frustration — why was one set of process specialists being paid 20% more than another *for doing the exact same type of work?* Needless to say, lackluster results were being delivered to clients. And because contracts were issued every three months for each individual project manager, this created an accounting headache for the company's support service personnel who handled contracts and payments.

IN WITH THE NEW

My consulting team saw this situation as a tremendous opportunity for cost savings and quality improvement. We challenged Barbara and her senior leadership team — a blended group of employees and contracted vendors — to come up with a system for vendor management that would result in an improvement of the quality of service and the CEO's 20% savings. Her team embraced the task and viewed it as a chance to reward exemplary vendors, reduce excessive paperwork involved for project support services, and save the company money.

Over the course of four months, my consulting team and Barbara's senior team developed a new vendor selection system. We began our process by identifying where the current system was struggling and failing. The team then examined the issues one-by-one and created a system that addressed the two major problem areas: contract personnel selection and service evaluation.

The new system consolidated the unwieldy pool of vendors down to only five vendors that were each extensively evaluated and deemed *qualified*. Next, those vendors were invited to *bid* on each open position; meaning, they could nominate an individual for each position by providing an outline of qualifications and salary requirements. Vendors were given *bid packages* that included job descriptions and strict procedures on how they were to submit all of the candidate and vendor information to the company. When vendors returned these bid packages, a committee evaluated each one via the same set of guidelines and awarded the positions to the best individuals proposed by the vendors.

Once the vendors were selected, each one was required to read and sign a standard *service level agreement*: a document that clearly outlined what was expected of each vendor in terms of their contribution to the company's projects. Customer service reviews were also implemented, and every quarter, vendors met with the company's management to perform a thorough review of their services and employees. Recognizing the need to boost motivation among vendors, my team recommended Barbara establish a bonus structure that would reward vendors who delivered consistently high marks in all areas of service. Finally, each position was re-bid only once a year, cutting back on unnecessary paperwork while still allowing for fresh perspectives and new talent to join the team.

Lipstick Leadership

"As a single mother I learned the value of planning ahead...planning big things. Back in 1976, I decided to celebrate the country's bicentennial with a cross-country (east to west coast and back) road trip with my four-year-old daughter. I invited a girlfriend with a six-year-old to join me. We planned the trip loosely on a small budget, loaded up my Toyota station wagon, and set off for an astonishing adventure. Plan it, do it, enjoy it learn and remember forever! It's the same thing in business!"

~ Esther Jantzen

The development of this simplified system was time-consuming and sometimes tedious; however, our commitment to improving the process for the future resulted in long-term rewards. In addition to providing Barbara's department with the highest quality vendors, this system saved the department over 25% in contract service costs — exceeding the corporate mandate by 5%. This system continues to save the corporation time and money and proves turning chaos into order is worth the effort.

MBA (Mom's Business Acumen) Class: What's Your System?

When you're feeling overwhelmed by chaos at work, implement a system to save time, money, and manpower. An organized and efficient system will help you take control and grow your organization.

Start by listing issues, projects or tasks for which you have been struggling to find a solution.

- ◆ Is there a project or task you dread?
- ◆ What tasks do you tend to put off?
- ◆ What tasks need other team members' skills, talents, and time to get the job done?
- ◆ What tasks can you do in a less expensive or more efficient way?
- ◆ What tasks can you put a timeline to?

Once you've established this list, assemble your team and provide them with following the seven steps below to help find the solution. You don't have to do it alone!

Seven Steps to Bringing Order to Your Chaos

Step 1: Describe the project you would like to organize.

Step 2: Write down where you are now with your project.

Step 3: Write down the end results you are looking for.

Step 4: List the steps to get to your end result. Write each step on its own index card and don't forget to use action words!

Step 5: On a blank surface, start arranging your index card tasks sequentially.

Step 6: Utilize "process map symbols" on each index card to indicate the flow of work:

- ◆ Oval = Beginning and end points

- ◆ Boxes or rectangles = A task or activity performed

- ◆ Diamonds = Point to the alternate outcomes of "yes/no" questions

- ◆ Arrows = Indicate the direction of work flow; used between index cards

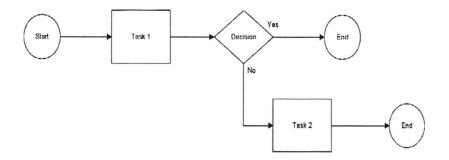

Step 7: Convert your information to a drawing that can be reproduced and handed out to the team

Go find the inefficiencies in your workplace and build a process to eliminate them. Then, like Marty, you can say good-by to chaos and hello to control!

CHAPTER 5

CLEANING HABITS OF LITTLE BOYS

MOM EXPERIENCE

In the previous stories, I've told you how my mom Mimi, my mother-in-law Marty and my Aunt Marie have influenced my management skills, but being a mother myself has also been a significant learning experience in my life and in my career. Being raised by and exposed to these amazing "moms" of mine has truly been a gift. At the time I'm writing this, I'm a few days away from sending my youngest son off to college, and I'm getting ready to embark on a whole new phase of parenting and personal development in my life. It seems appropriate that I'm reflecting back on what motherhood has meant to me and what I've learned from it.

Though I don't have twelve kids like my mother-in-law Marty or even five kids like my mother Mimi, I've learned PLENTY from my experiences raising my two children! My husband Rich and I have been married twenty-one years, and we have two sons: Michael and Kevin. We were planning on having four children, but complications with the delivery of my second son made it impossible for me to have any more children. At the time it was quite a blow, but my sons have brought me greater joy than I could've ever dreamed of.

BALANCING WORK AND HOME

Having the boys meant I needed to accept living in a very male dominated home, too, and as the only female, I play a very traditional role in the household. Thankfully, all of the cooking, cleaning, laundry and other typically "female" jobs in the house do not fall completely on my shoulders. My boys are very helpful, and my husband, Rich, is a fantastic partner.

Rich's realm has always been the construction and maintenance departments of running our household, but we would split the responsibilities of feeding, bathing and putting the boys to bed. I am fortunate to have a true partnership in my marriage and in household management. This boded well for our success as business partners in the creation of our management consulting firm, The Cove Group, Inc. We have been in business together for seven years which most people find pretty remarkable. But before our joint endeavor, I created my own home-based consulting firm and ran it successfully for ten years — while juggling my roles as wife, mother, and keeper of the house.

When Michael was born, I chose to leave my full-time job to stay home with him. Little did I know that three months after giving birth to him, I'd already be pregnant with my second son,

Lipstick Leadership

"My children taught me that sometimes everyone needs a nap and a snack! I try to remember that when I conduct long program meetings and begin to notice my staff's eyes start to glaze over...time to give them that nap (in the form of a break) and a snack!"

~ Mary Wright Benner, Program Director, The Conference Board

**Submit your best "Mom's Wisdom" story at
www.LipstickLeadership.com today!**

Kevin! Dealing with two babies was the toughest job I have ever held, but it was worth every second of it. Later when the boys were toddlers, I decided to start a home-based consulting business because I wanted to be there to experience every "first" with the boys and still develop my career. I was fortunate I had the type of business where I could do both.

During the day, I would take care of the house and the kids, and in the evenings I would drive my minivan with the kids strapped in their car seats to meet my husband in the parking lot of where he worked. We would exchange cars: he took the minivan (and the kids) and I would take his car on evening appointments with my clients. This was quite a sacrifice for my car-fanatic, neat-freak, mechanical engineering husband because my car was a typical "mom" car complete with Cheerios, baby pretzels, little trucks, G.I. Joe's, little army men and an incredible selection of children's music!

While I was home with the boys, I divided my time between caring for them and tending to the house. Cleaning was not my strong point, so I took a page out of Mimi's book and tried to recruit some help by making the cleaning a game for the boys. They've always been eager to pitch in — even though their help has sometimes been a little misguided.

NEW KIND OF WINDOW CLEANER

To say my sons' cleaning habits were interesting would be an understatement. Their male perspective on cleaning eclipsed even my standards. When it came time to help, the boys always liked to be involved. The first time they helped me wash windows, I wasn't even aware that they'd taken it upon themselves to lend a hand.

I had been cleaning for a couple of hours when I heard the front door open. My mother Mimi called out to me, her voice punctuated by laughter. As I came down the stairs, I heard her ask the boys what they were doing. I turned the corner into the living room to find them peering at me with innocent eyes and proud smiles. "Mommy, we were helping you wash the windows," they chimed. I looked over at the windows, and saw they looked very far from clean. Upon closer inspection, I discovered their surfaces were all wet and slimy!

My mother, hardly able to control her giggling, said to me, "Shelle, when I was walking up to the front door, I saw their sweet little faces through the window. They were spitting on the glass and rubbing it around with their hands!"

I wrinkled my nose, wondering what in the world would possess them to do that. Then I remembered: earlier in the day I had been washing a large picture window in the house, trying to wipe away the little handprints that get all over them. I would spray the window with cleaner and take my paper towel and rub away the grime, leaving the windows sparkling clean. Apparently, the boys watched me and thought that was a great idea. They decided they would help me and went to the windows by the front door and mimicked my movements; only, instead of cleaner, they used the only liquid they had: their spit! After wetting down the windows, they would move it around with their hands, "cleaning" the glass just like Mommy!

Though I was touched they wanted to help me, often the outcome of their assistance ended up producing *more* work for me rather than less. But I soon found that by gently guiding them in the right direction, I was able to focus their enthusiasm and energy more productively. Soon they were helping me reach all of my household cleanliness goals!

LOCKED OUT

My son Michael was physically precocious, climbing and running all over the house at ten months old while I, eight months pregnant at the time, waddled around after him trying to keep up. He was also fixated with "bad guys" and had a tendency to lock everything up to keep the "bad guys" out. Doors, cabinets, windows, containers, etc. — Michael helped out by making sure everything was always locked.

At that time, we lived in upstate New York in a one-story flat and in order to do our laundry, I had to go out the back door and re-enter the basement through a common door. One day, Mike was taking a nap so I shuffled down the stairs to do another load of laundry. When I came back to our door, it was locked! I tried not to panic, fighting those pesky pregnancy hormones and telling myself Mike was fine and most likely still sleeping. I dropped the laundry basket and ran to the windows to see if they were open. The first window was locked up tight, and through the panes, I could see Mike playing quietly in the living room with his trucks. While I was in the basement, he must have woken up, seen the door ajar and locked it like a good little boy trying to keep the "bad guys" out!

Mike looked up, smiled at me, waved and went back to playing. I tapped on the window trying to make him go to the back door and let Mommy in, but apparently, unlocking the door didn't make sense to this ten-month-old! After checking four other windows, I hit the jackpot with number five. I must have been quite a sight climbing in through that window, my big belly making it quite a tight fit! As I toppled inside, Mike took my hand and led me to the door to show me his handiwork. He not only locked the door but had pushed the highchair over, climbed up and fastened the chain, too. No bad guys were getting into our apartment today…and apparently no mommies either!

Lipstick Leadership

"In my own career in nursing, I was always impressed with those fellow nurses who constantly performed under stressful life-and-death situations. Having been exposed to a variety of such time sensitive situations where many diverse groups of individuals required immediate assistance, I learned the importance of correct and thorough intervention while being sensitive to their needs..."

~ Kati Machtley, Women's Summit Director, Bryant University

Advance your career with the help of Michelle's FREE e-zine. Sign up today at www.LipstickLeadership.com!

DADDY'S SHINGLING SURPRISE

Kevin's brand of helping was less technical and more physical. I remember Rich arriving home from work one evening and getting ready to finish shingling the outside our first little home.

As I was preparing dinner, I heard deep, low laughter coming from the other side of the kitchen wall. My husband called my name, and as I walked out of the house, five-year-old Kevin came running up behind me yelling, "Daddy saw my surprise!"

Rich was standing by the wall admiring Kevin's surprise: the very bottom row of newly installed shingles had about a hundred nails banged into it! Earlier that week when Rich was working on the house, Kevin insisted on helping him. So Rich set up a "work bench" for Kevin: two cinder blocks and a two-by-four strip of wood. He then asked Kevin to help him by putting as many nails into that piece of would that would fit. He handed Kevin a hammer, and Kevin happily went to work, banging away for days working on that project. I just assumed that the banging I'd heard all afternoon was just Kevin working on his special project. Little did I know, Kevin had determined the first project was done and it was time to help Daddy out more with the shingling! What a great surprise it would be for Daddy, Kevin thought, if he put nails in all the shingles. And he was absolutely right! His shingling escapade is also another example of great intention pointed in the wrong direction.

Simple Truth from Mom:
Make sure your team's energy is pointed in the same direction and working toward the same goal!

It occurred to me over time that my boys' energy and enthusiasm were a good thing! They wanted to help, God bless their little hearts. The only thing missing in these escapades was guidance — which I was responsible for providing.

> By focusing their energy in a helpful and fun direction, it could maybe mean less work for me instead of more. Every team needs this guidance. The most energetic team you can assemble will be the least productive if everyone is pulling in a different direction.

BUT WHAT DO YOU DO?

Recently, I was speaking about strategic planning for entrepreneurial success to a group of CEOs at a conference in Chicago. After my program, I was approached by one of the attendees, Sharon. Sharon is the CEO and president of a small company that reaches around $4M a year in revenue. She and her company had been trying to break the $5M mark for the past two years with no luck. After complimenting me on my program, she asked if she could buy me lunch and "pick my brain."

We went to grab a bite to eat and she began to tell me about her company. At first I thought she was in the consulting business…then the advertising business…wait, the healthcare business…or maybe it was graphic design? I began to get a headache trying to follow where she and her company were going. She thought the obstacle to her $5M goal was that her team was not executing their work effectively. "How can I motivate them, Michelle?" she asked.

As I started to draw a picture of her business model on a napkin, it became clear to me what her *real* issue was: Sharon could not clearly tell me in one sentence where her money came from! She had no idea what the mission of her business was or even give me a concise description of what they do. Her approach to date had been: tell me what you need, and I'll tell you how I can help you. Marketing, design, insurance — she was all over the place! And I thought I could safely assume her sales team and the processes of her company were equally as scattered.

DIRECTING YOUR TEAM

Sharon was making one of the worst mistakes an entrepreneur can make: she was ignoring the *real* problem barring her from greater success. It wasn't a lack of motivation that was keeping her team from reaching their $5M goal; it was a lack of clear direction. She was blaming her team for not all pulling in the same direction to hit the mark, *but she was the one who was giving them all of the different directions to follow!*

Lipstick Leadership

"Motherhood has taught me to keep things in perspective. When my children were younger and I'd be in the middle of a work crisis, the moment I got home and held one of my children and saw the look in their eyes as they talked to me, the big crisis just became a situation that had to be dealt with rather than an all-consuming problem taking over every single ounce of my energy and thought. My children keep me grounded and balanced. That is a necessary skill in my work — as well as a necessary atti-

tude to possess — always keep things in perspective. Being able to step back from a situation, accurately access it, weighing out pros and cons, obstacles, challenges and options prior to coming to a conclusion is critical. Having said that, I still struggle with not reacting to the moment but being a mother has taught me to be more patient, open-minded, flexible and wise!!"

~ Rita Allen, Rita B. Allen Associates

Submit your best "Mom's Wisdom" story at www.LipstickLeadership.com today!

Without clear direction from management on what the business is, what the goals are, and what role each person plays in meeting those goals, the team cannot be held accountable for the lackluster outcomes that follow. Just as I wasn't able to direct my boys until I recognized that it was I who was not providing good leadership, the results of Sharon's sales team were scattered because she didn't provide them with a clear and focused target. A revenue number alone was not enough to build a strategic sales program.

After our lunch, Sharon wasn't really any closer to reaching $5M in revenues; however, she now understood the initial step to hitting that goal was for her to determine the identity of her company and then communicate it clearly to her team. She booked a series of coaching sessions, and we worked on sorting out what she wanted from her business, where her intellectual talent lay, and where her money would come from in a clear and sustained and repetitive fashion. She shed the parts of her business that were not producing enough of a profit margin and rededicated resources to the parts of her business that had a high margin and potential for growth.

When we developed a sales funnel and a plan for selling strategies for her team, everyone was now pulling in the same direction. No one was spitting on any windows…including Sharon!

MBA (Mom's Business Acumen) Class: Getting Your Team Pulling Together

Before you can determine if your team is pulling in the right direction toward growth, you need to have a clear picture of your business — mission, vision and values — and specific processes and systems in place. Once you can breakdown and analyze your process, you can pinpoint where your team might need a tweak or adjustment.

Whether you're starting a new team or managing an existing one, how do you get everyone to act like a team and move in the same direction toward success?

1. Clearly define roles, goals and responsibilities. Everybody needs to understand what their role is and how it's an integral piece of the big picture.

2. Find a supportive and knowledgeable manager or leader for the team. Someone has to be able to lead this diverse group and keep everyone on-task and in-line with the

goals at hand. Without a strong leader, it's easy for a team to lose sight of project goals.

3. Respect the different talents of your team members. Those different skill sets and talents are what will make the team successful — if you know how to handle team members whose talents might clash with each other. By clearly defining roles, goals and responsibilities (#1), you can avoid skirmishes between, for instance, the creative free-flowing member and the analytical organized member.

4. Promote — nay, DEMAND open and honest communication among all team members. This is a critical must-have for a high-functioning team. Continually sharing information and insights will ensure everyone is on the same page of the project.

5. Make sure the leader has the authority to make decisions. Without some level of authority, the team will quickly begin to feel like they are just spinning their wheels. What's the use in coming up with great ideas if you can't implement them? That's the fastest way to frustrate a team.

6. Implement a reward or recognition plan. When the team has accomplishments or when individuals in the team have accomplished their portion of a job, they need to be recognized for their contribution. One of the major fears that keep people from working in teams is that working in a team will diminish their personal achievements. Rewarding a team as a whole and recognizing each individual's contributions will develop harmony within the team.

Pick one of these ideas and implement it today…but remember: no spitting on someone else's windows!

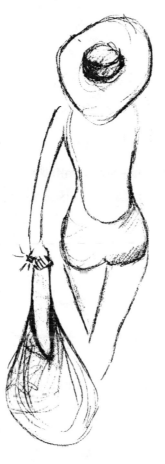

CHAPTER 6

WEAR YOUR DIAMONDS TO THE BEACH

THE SHERMAN HISTORY

My mother's side of my family, the Shermans, are a stark contrast to the Italian immigrants of my father's side of the family, the Yozzos. The Shermans were statesman and among the founders of America. They were politicians and therefore, influencers of public policy. My ancestor, Roger Sherman, was a signer of the Declaration of Independence and the Constitution, and my great-great-grandfather James Schoolcraft Sherman was Vice President of the United States (I have an amazing dress that was worn to the inaugural ball by my great-great-grandmother).

To say the way my mother's family lived was different from my father's family life is quite an understatement! The way these two families collide together in my parents' marriage is part of what

Lipstick Leadership

"My mother taught me to be real — never to lose who I am in the work environment. It has served me well the past thirty-two years with IBM where, in the beginning, high heels were an unusual sight. My ability to be authentic has helped me create a career that is rewarding and challenging and suited perfectly to ME!"

~ Nancy DeViney, Vice President of Values and Organizational Capacity, IBM makes me who I am. The contrast in how each family sees the world and what each expects from different situations has had a profound influence on me. The push and pull of these relationships has made me able to look at things with a larger vision and an understanding of the hard work necessary to accomplish that vision.

My maternal grandmother was Frances Snyder Sherman, or "Mops" as I called her, a playful name for a woman who was gruff and stern in her demeanor. Growing up, Mops split her time between a penthouse across the street from the Waldorf Astoria in Manhattan and a grand estate in Rye, New York. Her childhood was one of affluence and privilege, boarding schools, maids and nannies — very different from my childhood! She was the youngest of three girls born to Louie Snyder and Gertrude Ahles Snyder. Great-grandpa Louie, who wanted a boy, treated Mops like the son he never had. She was raised to be tough, critical, outspoken and an athlete. She never viewed herself as particularly feminine — that was her sister's and mother's job.

GOLFING IN THE 1920s

As the "son" in the family, Mops was called Frankie, and at almost six feet tall, she projected a confidence she never really felt on the inside. She was very modest regarding her own abilities and talents right up to the end. Groomed by her overbearing father to be a champion golfer, she was dominating the golf circuit by the time she was a teenager. She even won the father/son tournaments Louie entered them in. When she was old enough to tour on her own, Mops became a member of an elite group of affluent female golfers, including Patty Berg and Babe Zaharias, who later founded the LPGA. In those days, the early to mid 1920s, women were not allowed to stay in hotels, so they were hosted by prominent families who belonged to the country clubs where the women were golfing.

It was in Utica, New York at the Yahnundasis Country Club, when Mops was being hosted by the Sherman family that she met my grandfather and her life changed. The father of her host was Vice President of the United States, James Schoolcraft Sherman, and the Shermans had a son close to Mop's age, James Schoolcraft Sherman III. Jim was immediately taken with my grandmother. He was gentle and playful and made young Mops feel feminine. He softened her disposition and outlook on life. For the first time, she felt like a woman.

After the tournament, the golfers were off to another city, and Mops and Jim said goodbye to each other. But to Mops' surprise, Jim showed up at the next tournament...and then the next. Jim traveled all over the country pursuing my grandmother until she agreed to marry him and leave golf for family life in upstate New York. When she married my grandfather, she became a wife and then a mother, although she was much more comfortable with the "little creatures" once they were big enough to play with. Pops drew out the softer side of Mops. As a mother, Mops was the disciplinarian. Without the physical outlet of golf, she took to the more physical tasks around the home, like playing games with the kids and doing outdoor chores like raking and shoveling, very unusual for a woman of her status in life. She was strict but fair, always involved philanthropically and with the children's activities (especially if they involved athletics), but she continued to have a hard time expressing her emotions.

THE GOLFING "SOCIALITE"

Mops was a non-traditional grandmother figure in my childhood, a strange mix of gruff and playful. Pops died when I was just five years old, breaking my grandmother's heart and widowing her at a young age. Mops always said golf saved her life after Pops died. After losing the love of her life and the only person who made her feel like a woman, Mops sold the family home. I was seven years old when she moved into the condo on the golf course in North Carolina. She lived there the remaining years of her life with the exception of the last few when she was confined to a nursing home. That move to North Carolina meant that for the first time, she was on her own: no parents, no husband, and no servants. She had to take care of herself, and she explored scrubbing pots and pans, cleaning the kitchen and bathrooms, gardening on her balcony, cooking, and doing the laundry, all with gusto.

Lipstick Leadership

"I learned confidence. Not just from my mother, but [from] my father as well. My mother did not work outside of the home for much of my life, but she was a certified teacher of Home Economics. She was good

at her job, looking after us. If we had a problem at school, she took care of it. When I was denied the chance to take Shop Class, my mother went to the school to talk to the administrators. If my father was needed, they would go together on a second trip. I was a third child — second trips were not required. I took Shop."

~ Cynthia Wood, Director of Facilities Maintenance
   & Engineering – Ann Arbor Campus, Pfizer

**Submit your best "Mom's Wisdom" story at
www.LipstickLeadership.com today!**

Mops was also an unusual and non-traditional socialite. She never had to work a day in her life so she spent her free time golfing. She had such strength on the golf course; she could out drive any man I knew and only played from the men's tees until she was well into her 80s. On my wedding day, she played golf with my father, brother, uncles and future husband. My grandmother walked in places men walked because her father expected it of her.

MOPS' DIAMOND RING

My relationship with Mops more closely resembled a relationship with a grandfather than a grandmother. The one truly feminine thing that stuck out about Mops was a large sparkly ring that was always present on her right ring finger. This ring was unique; it was the size and shape of a postage stamp with a square diamond in the middle with a cluster of diamonds surrounding it. There were only two designed and created in the entire world, and the other ring was given to Bess Truman. The ring was handed down to Mops from her Aunt Virginia Ahles.

I never remember seeing Mops without that ring on. It stood out to me because the style seemed so out of character for Mops. Except for her wedding ring and a watch, it was the only jewelry she ever wore. Mops' style was very masculine, and she often shopped in the men's department and in golf pro shops. No matter what she was doing — gardening or washing dishes — or what she was wearing — men's pants and button-down shirts — she wore that ring, even when she was doing something really active or messy like combing the beaches for shells. I learned later that her ring represented the best of who she was as a woman.

She even wore that ring playing golf until it was stolen one day. She was up on the green, putting, when a man came out of the woods and swiped her ditty bag containing Aunt V.'s ring, her wedding ring, and watch. Mops saw him and hunted him down. She eventually found the items at a pawn shop where she bought them back. After that, she left her valuables at home when she headed off to the golf course. But that was about the only time that she didn't wear her ring.

The fact that she always wore that ring and didn't put it away in a box only for special occasions requiring "dressy" clothes taught me a valuable lesson: always bring everything you've got into whatever you're doing; don't save it all up for later.

I asked Mops why she wore that ring all the time because it seemed awfully dressed up to me. She told me not to be afraid to show my gifts. Her ring was her treasure. It was something that reminded her of all that it means to be a woman. It reminded her of her family. It kept her connected to the women of her past and to my grandfather. She felt that although her time with him was brief, she was her best as a woman with him. Mops encouraged me NOT to keep my beautiful things for that elusive "special day" that may never come. She taught me to use them every day.

Simple Truth from Mom:
Don't wait until the eleventh hour to
let your ideas shine... don't be afraid to
show off your "diamonds!"

My grandmother brought her A-game to everything she did, and she wore her diamonds no matter what, whether it was playing golf or growing her plants on her balcony or playing with her children. She knew how to commit to life full steam ahead.

At work your talent, ideas and skills are your diamonds. Many of us hold onto our brilliant ideas for just the right person or just the right time. Do you have amazing ideas that might never get executed? Well, *what are you waiting for??* Like Mops, wear YOUR diamonds every single day!

THE MESSENGER SYNDROME

Many employees spend a tremendous amount of time and energy worrying about what the boss thinks about them, their performance, and their ideas. But they neglect to think about how their work impacts the business' bottom line. If they did think about their impact, I'm sure they would be braver about how they communicate up-line to their boss. Most people are afraid to give the boss bad news, even if they have a solution for the problem. They work off of the "kill the messenger" fear and figure that someone else will let the boss know about the problem anyway.

I spend a lot of my coaching hours dedicated to helping clients "find the words" to approach their superiors with problems and overcome their fear to be able to present their innovative ideas on how to solve the issues. I help them get brave enough to share their troubleshooting brilliance and show off their "diamonds!"

LETTING "DIAMOND" IDEAS SHINE

One of my clients, Jane, an insurance saleswoman, was struggling with how to communicate with her boss Jeff. Jeff had developed quite a reputation among his colleagues for having an explosive temper and for berating teammates who told him things he didn't want to hear. Unfortunately for Jane, she had some bad news to deliver: her department had been tasked with developing three new products for the company and they were already five weeks behind the schedule, due to some IT problems. Jane had a solution for keeping this delay from impacting the company's bottom line, but it was a radical idea that would involve a fair amount of risk. Should she bravely forge ahead and present this idea to the volatile Jeff, or should she stand back and let someone else figure out a solution?

In a panic, Jane called me for an emergency onsite session. We had been working together over the phone for months, developing ways to advance her career and find greater satisfaction in her work. I knew this must be serious if she was willing to foot the bill for a day-long session with me at her office in New York City! So I hopped on a train from my office in Connecticut and on the way, I reviewed Jane's file to familiarize myself with her situation. I wanted to understand the issue and the options for solutions, and I needed to be fully aware of Jane's strengths so we could work on an approach to communicate her idea to Jeff. I also looked at her previous comments about Jeff — stories of how he interacted with her colleagues — to get a better understanding of how others had succeeded or failed in communicating with him.

Lipstick Leadership

"I learned from a friend's mom that it is never too late to start afresh or mentally wipe a slate clean and give yourself a new chance to do what you want to do and be who you want to be. This friend's mom battled alcoholism successfully when I was in high school. She emerged as such a strong person and such a role model. Not that she drew attention to herself for accomplishing what she did, but her example — her actions — have reminded me time

and again to look forward, and not feel mired in a path suggested by the past."

~ Regina Maruca, Former Harvard Business Review Editor and Co-Author of "The Leadership Legacy"

Advance your career with the help of Michelle's FREE e-zine. Sign up today at www.LipstickLeadership.com!

I arrived at Jane's office armed with information and a few ideas for various plans to deal with this dilemma strategically. After I helped her convince herself that her brilliant idea was worth the risk, we holed up in her office for the afternoon, creating a foolproof presentation for Jeff. All the evidence indicated that he was a very direct, to-the-point person, so I focused on helping Jane deliver her message with brevity and plenty of facts rather than a lot of "beating around the bush" and opinions. Together, we crafted a 3-slide presentation, a one-page report and a list of major talking points. When I left her office, she was ready to let her "diamond" idea shine!

PITCHING TO THE BOSS

The next day, Jane told several of her teammates she was planning on presenting a new idea to Jeff. The overall consensus was:

"Jane, you're crazy!" They tried to talk her out of it, claiming Jeff wouldn't listen to the problem, let alone her solution to it. But Jane could not be dissuaded. She decided her idea was important to the business, and if she focused on how she could help, instead of her fear, she was confident Jeff would see its merit.

At the appointed time, Jane walked into Jeff's office and utilized her talent, industry-knowledge and the strategy we developed to get her points across. She briefly explained the problem and then launched right into her idea on how to fix it, not giving Jeff the chance to have a fit over the situation. Because of the confidence she had in her idea and the way she presented it, Jeff was open to her idea. He was actually thankful for her frankness and creativity regarding the issue, and in the end, he fully supported her recommendation. From that point on, Jane didn't hesitate to bring forth her amazing ideas and innovative solutions. And what did this commitment to always bringing her A-game earn Jane besides a few words of praise from her boss? A new position…two levels up in the organization!

MBA (Mom's Business Acumen) Class: Tips to Pitch Your Idea

Have you ever sat in a meeting and had a co-worker present a fantastic solution to the boss — the same solution you were thinking about but were too afraid to say aloud? They obviously didn't steal your idea, but it's hard not to get angry when all the praise and glory goes to the co-worker who brought the idea forward. But rather than directing that anger at your co-worker — or even yourself for staying silent — use the moment to reflect on what's keeping you from bringing your ideas forward. Understanding what barriers are holding you back can help you be brave enough to speak up and share your talent in the future.

Here are some questions to ask yourself if you're hesitant to share your brilliance:

1. **Do you feel everything needs to be perfect before you can take action?** If your perfectionism is driving you crazy...I hate to tell you this, but it's probably driving everyone else in the office crazy, too. Perfectionism can hold you back because it paralyzes you. It keeps you from getting your ideas out because you feel like your presentation is never perfect enough to get pitched to your boss. Understanding WHY you feel everything needs to be perfect before it leaves your desk is important.

2. **Do you have a fear of being judged or having your idea rejected?** What happens if you put your idea out there...and the boss thinks it's stupid or someone else pokes holes in it? How strongly do you believe in the impact your solution could have for the company? How hard are you willing to fight for that positive outcome? The answers should give you the strength to put yourself on the line. There are always going to be "hole-pokers" out there, people that can find something wrong with your plan, and that's good. Those people will help you refine your plan so that it becomes a *successful* plan.

3. **Are you too shy to say your idea out loud?** When you have an introverted personality you might have a hard time standing up and having any attention focused on you. A lot of times that means the amazing things floating around in your head just stay in there. What a shame

that the company never benefits by those diamond ideas! If you can't seem to get past your shyness, work on pushing past those fears and in the meantime, find a buddy who can be the salesperson of your ideas. If you make sure your buddy gives you your due credit, that partnership could be great for both of you. Go find the yin to your yang and you both get to shine!

4. **Are you afraid of risk?** Does the fear of the unknown paralyze you? If you don't want to do anything unless you feel it's a sure thing, you could be in danger of hiding your diamonds. You'll be destined to be one of the soldiers in your workplace, caught in execution for ever. If you want to lead, then you have to know that there is a degree of risk that goes along with the job. Leaders have to take risks because the decision-making responsibility is on their shoulders.

So get comfortable with risk. Come out of your shell or buddy up. Don't be afraid of judgment or rejection: use it to strengthen your plans and ideas. Know that perfectionism holds you back, and ALWAYS bring your A-game. Bring on the brilliance!

CHAPTER 7

BIG SISTER, LITTLE MOM

THE WOMAN IN THE SHOE

We all know the nursery rhyme about the woman in the shoe, "she had so many children she didn't know what to do!" I think Marty Drake's house must have surely felt like that shoe, filled to brim with children, dogs, horses and a husband. I have been blessed with knowing amazing women throughout my life; some by blood, by friendship and in Marty Drake's case, by marriage. To this day, I have no idea how she successfully managed such a household, and I am thankful to have married into her family and learn from the stories that make up the fabric of growing up in the Drake household.

WHAT IS NORMAL?

When my husband Rich describes his childhood, it sounds like this: "When I think about how I grew up, it doesn't sound unusual to me — maybe to a lot of other people, but not to me." Remember, Rich is one of twelve kids. He has five brothers and six sisters (which means I have a lot of in-laws!). With a span of only fourteen years from the oldest to the youngest child, there was quite a clutter of people in the Drake household, but none of them ever saw the size of their family as an issue. It was just the way it was. And while the Drakes were an even split by the numbers, the feminine influence was strong, VERY strong. There is nothing better than a strong woman, and the Drake women all have strong personalities — none of them are pushovers.

Marty and her clan lived in a six-bedroom house. The six girls were paired up in rooms according to age, Marty and Stan had the master bedroom and there were two rooms left for the boys. At one point, they were arranged five in one bedroom with two bunk beds and a crib. To say living arrangements were tight would be an understatement! And there always seemed to be some construction project going on that displaced someone. The reason why Marty had to implement her "towels and toothpaste" plan was because the other bathroom in the house was being remodeled and so there was only that one bathroom for all fourteen to share!

Marty had to cook, shop, launder, organize and clean for everybody. She had all of the day-to-day duties all of us moms are responsible for, but imagine doing that for a brood that size. Simple things like cooking pancakes for the children for breakfast is no big deal for me with my two teenage sons and a husband, but when you're trying to cook pancakes for over a dozen people, it becomes a much bigger operation — an operation that required a team! Every meal, every day was complex, but Marty always did a great job, and now that all of her children have children, there is an even greater level of appreciation among the Drake kids for her tremendous act of raising all of them.

DINNER WITH THE DRAKES

Marty ran a very structured and disciplined house, and I suspect that it was by necessity she was that way with all of those children running around. Dinnertime was very important to the Drakes because Marty believed they should sit down as a family every night, and she had rules the children had to abide by in order to make dinner a pleasant experience. If you didn't sit down with the family at the appointed hour, you didn't get anything to eat. If a child was pinching or poking a sibling at the table, they had to sit on the hand they were not using to eat. Most nights ended will all of the boys sitting on one hand and quickly eating with the other...before a brother stole a meatball. While telling me this story, Rich recalled with a laugh that it wasn't until college that he finally got to eat with both hands on the table! Entertaining was not a common occurrence, but every now and then a Drake child would slip in a friend at the dinner table. A guest would go virtually unnoticed until dessert when Marty would count of the number of plates needed to put cake on the table in front of everyone, and when she counted out more than fourteen, she noticed the stowaway.

Lipstick Leadership

"My mother's mother, whom we called Grandma, always made people feel appreciated — whether it was the painter, the butcher or the meter reader. When I served as Executive Director of a non-profit organization for ten years, I often heard from volunteers about how they felt appreciated in the organization. I wrote frequent thank you notes, celebrated volunteers with an annual potluck dinner, highlighted people's generosity (of time and money) in our newsletters and annual reports, and always made sure they knew how much their contributions meant to the organization. While I probably spent a good part of my time thanking people, in the long run, it supported a very loyal group of volunteers. Thank you, Grandma, for showing me the power of appreciating people."

~ Lisa Tener, Book Coach

**Submit your best "Mom's Wisdom" story at
www.LipstickLeadership.com today!**

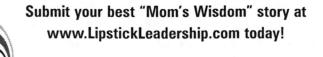

When Rich and I were first dating, I was invited over for dinner. Now at the dinner table at my parent's house, there were always a few conversations going on at once. My loud boisterous Italian family never had a quiet meal; we carried on multiple and usually passionate discussions all at the same time. The rule was whoever spoke the loudest had the floor, and we all had our turns to share our news and opinions! So at Marty's, as dinner started there were about nine of us sitting around the table, and I immediately started the conversation ball rolling. When I asked Marty how she met Stan, Rich and his siblings stared at me gape-mouthed as if I had asked what type of birth control she used! As Marty happily told me the story of how the huge family got started, you could hear a pin drop. I found out later was that you could always hear a pin drop at mealtime at the Drakes because there was only one conversation allowed at a time, and 99% of the time it was between Stan and Marty. Rather than Marty and Stan having to referee the conversations of all the kids, the children were often silent. That shocked look on their faces was because I initiated a conversation. Later, Rich told me that he learned more about his parents from that one story Marty told me at dinner than he had learned in all the years growing up in his house.

CHORES AT THE DRAKE HOUSE

Keeping a large family organized and functioning was no small task. Marty assigned the chores, and all the children pitched in. She posted a monthly calendar on the refrigerator, and each child would end up rotating through all the chores — that way no one could complain so-and-so always got the easy jobs! This schedule was also set in stone: no negotiation, no arguments. It included all of the day-to-day activities needed to run the household like washing dishes, clearing the table, cleaning the kitchen, and sweeping the dining room floor. The kids worked in pairs to increase efficiency. Rich was partnered with his older brother Joe, and on Mondays they washed the dishes. Yikes! No dishwasher! On Tuesdays Tommy and Willie would wash; Wednesday was Chrissy and Loraine's day…you get the picture!

The one chore that was guarded by Marty was the laundry. She never let the children touch her washing machine; the few times someone did, the machine always broke, and when it did, it was disaster! Marty would have to pile everything in the back of a pickup truck to transport it to the Laundromat to clean, and a trip like that could break the bank. So Marty and her magic touch with the machines would put in the wash, transfer it to the dryer and pile it on the table in their laundry room. It was then the responsibility of the girls to fold it, separate it and bring it to each of their siblings' rooms.

The girls were also responsible for cleaning bathrooms, vacuuming and dusting. But the boys didn't get off easy: they were responsible for shoveling snow in the winter, mowing the lawn, painting the house, fixing windows and various other repairs that needed to be done around the house and yard. Marty also smartly assigned specific tasks to children who had the talents and skills to do them and do them well. When Rich was ten-years–old, he was tuning up the cars, fixing the flat tires and changing the oil and brakes because that was his aptitude and interest.

Although Marty ran a very traditional household in terms of male/female responsibility, she still taught her sons how to cook and clean. None of the men in her family were going to shy away from cooking or cleaning as adults. I have enjoyed some of my favorite meals at my brother-in-law Bob's house, and I would put him up against any chef from any day of the week. When I travel to speak at conferences, my boys never have to worry about what they might eat; Rich is an amazing cook as well. Big thanks go out to Marty for teaching *all* of her kids how to cook!

A LEADER EMERGES

When I look at a business's organization chart, I see the structure of the employees in relation to the outcomes they are trying to achieve. If I were to apply a business structure to my mother-in-law's household, the initial assumption would be that she ran a very flat organization: one leader with a dozen employees all reporting to her, each positioned to execute simple tasks in a complex environment. With all the moving parts of this large household and the need for everyone to pitch in, managing this team would be a challenge for even the most seasoned business executive. Industry standards often dictate leaders should have no more than eight people directly reporting to them…and here's Marty with *twelve* direct reports: her frontline workers — the Drake kids: Terri, Pat, Bob, Marcia, Tom, Willie, Joe, Chrissie, Rich, Charlotte, Loraine, and Matt — all reporting directly to the CEO: Marty! It was only natural that a leader would immerge internally.

Each child had a birth order number that defined the type of experience they had in the household growing up. Rich is the ninth child of the twelve, and his sister Pat was number two. Marty was pregnant most of my sister-in-law Pat's childhood; she was not only pregnant, but chasing around infants, toddlers, and teenagers.

With everything Marty needed to do each day, she had to have help. But help comes in two different forms. There was the begrudging help you do because your mom asked you or told you to do it, and there is the help that comes unexpectedly. That kind of help comes along because someone notices something that needs to be done and that person just takes the initiative and does it. Pat Drake Snyder offered that kind of help to Marty and just picked up the reins and emerged as a leader in her mother's home.

A LITTLE BOY'S MEMORIES

My sister-in-law Pat and I have always been close. I don't know if it is because we are both artists, or if it's how our personalities compliment each other. But I think it may be largely because she played such an important role in my husband Rich's early development. .

Rich doesn't have the clearest recollections from his early childhood, but the things he does remember doing, like riding a two-wheeler for the first time and ice skating for the first time, he always remembers doing with Pat. When asked about his relationship with Pat, Rich replied:

> "First off, I love all my siblings. I have strong, positive childhood memories of each one — the games we would play together, the days at the beach spent together, the holiday banter, and the times we rallied together when someone needed help. But just like every other family on the planet, we didn't — and still don't — always get along. Each one of us has a strong personality, and we believe what we believe, always with

conviction. It's natural the bonds between us tend to vary in strength over the years. Sometimes the bonds are quite strong; other times not so much. But there is one sibling with whom I have always felt strongly connected — my second oldest sister, Pat. Every memory I have of Pat is a positive one. I simply cannot think of an instance when I felt angry at Pat or hardly even slightly annoyed.

"It wasn't until we grew up and started our own families that I realized why the bond with Pat was so strong, why the memories are nothing but positive. Pat was my second mom! With my mom so busy with the day-to-day chores and chasing after the 'three little kids', she simply didn't have time to keep all twelve of us in line (Charlotte, Loraine and Matt have always been — even to this day — the 'three little kids'. There was a two year gap between me and Charlotte, which allowed me to avoid being the *fourth* little kid). Pat just seemed to naturally fit the role of my second mom. Among many memories, I vividly remember when she took me ice skating for the first time. It occurs to me now that she was a teenaged girl at the time but had no problem taking her snot-nosed little brother along. In later years she gently guided me down a path towards being a caring adult. She was always selfless, patient and nurturing — a natural mother."

Pat always found the time to devote to her little brother so he could experience some of the simple pleasures of childhood that might have otherwise gotten lost in the shuffle. Pat stepped up to the plate when Marty and Stan Drake just simply didn't have the time to go and help each of their children to do all of these things they wanted to. Today, kids are driven to baseball games, softball games, karate class, piano lessons and much more. But it simply wasn't possible to do with so many kids. Even logistically: there wasn't a vehicle big enough to cart everyone (unless you count the bus Marty drove for the school district) or enough time to be everywhere at once. But Pat selflessly donated her time to help out, allowing Rich to have those experiences, and in the process helped shape who he is today.

Lipstick Leadership

"The best lesson Mom taught me and I have taught many of my girlfriends is you can't get everything you need from just one person. Our spouses do not give us everything we need; they don't want to see chick flicks or try on new clothes. That's why we need girlfriends. I have also applied it where I work. Some people are fun to work with and enhance your day...but may not be best to delegate work to...but they help you keep your sanity in the workplace. Some are great workers and you can count on them to make your job easier.

Some are great leaders and role models helping bring direction to the work environment. It takes them all to make your job work."

~ Sheila Smith, High School Business Teacher

There's no better example of Pat's influence than an incident that happened one summer when Rich was only five- or six-years-old. The children used to play a game called "Spud." It's a yard game where everyone stands in a circle, and in the center, the person who's "it" calls out someone's name and throws a rubber ball in the air. The person whose name is called has to catch the ball while everyone else runs away. When the ball is caught, everyone freezes, and the person with the ball throws it and tries to hit the nearest person. If that person is hit by the ball, he or she gets and "S" and he or she has to throw the ball next; if they miss getting hit, the thrower gets an "S" and has to throw the ball again. When you've been hit enough times to spell the word *spud*, you're out; the winner is the person who has the least letters.

Can you picture those twelve wild Drakes running around the front yard yelling and screaming and taunting each other! During a game one day, Rich yelled at his sister, "FAT PAT" and laughed at his own silliness before noticing Pat suddenly left the game and went inside. Rich then realized what he said was mean and might have hurt Pat's feelings, and he felt absolutely horrible about it. He immediately stopped playing the game and went in to apologize to Pat. She reassured him she was fine and that she didn't go inside because of what he had said. She gave him a big hug and told him she appreciated he was concerned about how she felt. To have such an effect on a little boy, that he was so concerned about the feelings of someone else at such a young age, is a tribute to the connection Pat and Rich had. Their bond and the reason he was able to comfortably go to her and apologize was a direct result of her influence on him in those early years. And as Rich's wife, his ability to apologize is a trait I am forever grateful to Pat for cultivating in him!

PAT'S LEADERSHIP STYLE

As I said earlier, my sisters-in-law all have strong personalities. I don't think Pat is an exception, but although her personality is strong, it is so in a different way. I see her strength in terms of who she is and how she interacts with others. Her strength of character and her resolve make it so she isn't a pushover, but that strength is balanced by her tendencies to nurture. While she may not be boisterous, she is playful in a gentle and caring way. Rich credits a major part of his development as a person to her influence, and because of her, he is warm, caring and understanding. Remembering how Pat treated her much younger brother, he draws on that influence and has always been a favorite with young children — everyone always says he has the magic touch with crying babies!

We as women have the ability to influence everyone in our lives, and when we do, we pass on our traits to those we influence. I know Pat's daughter Kristen will pass that torch of positive influence her mother passed on to her and in turn pass it on to the children in her classroom.

Simple Truth from Mom:
Leaders emerge from all levels of an organization and can influence everyone from the top to the bottom

Pat showed her influence and leadership by taking on additional responsibilities with the raising of her siblings and later with the raising of her own children. She was never instructed to go take care of her brothers and sisters, and her leadership was natural. Marty may have had the ultimate decision making authority, but Pat was given a lot of free rein.

She took the lesson that she could be a leader no matter where she was in an organization from her mother's kitchen all the way to her own corner office. But, now it's YOUR turn! Be a leader everyday whether you're the CEO or the assistant to the CEO, and create the same kind of positive influence in your workplace that Pat did in her mother's home.

BEING A COACH-IN-LAW

My relationship with my sister-in-law Pat took a professional turn when Pat decided she wanted to return to work after raising her children. She was an art teacher by trade and had been the lead teacher for the Riverhead, Long Island Gifted and Talented afterschool and summer enrichment program. But the market was not very open for teachers at that time. After being out of the workforce for a while, Pat came to me for guidance. She asked me to review her resume and give her a little sisterly coaching on the interview process.

After analyzing her resume and speaking with her at length about her experience and her aspirations, I found many of her traits and skills would be applicable in the workplace outside the educational arena. When Pat was teaching in New York, she also ran many cultural activities like local art shows to highlight her students' work. When she revealed this to me, my eyes lit up like I had found a pot of gold! Rather than focusing on her experience in the field of education, we began to redesign Pat's resume to highlight the skills she utilized to run those huge events. We also worked on Pat's communication strategy so she would be able to easily and concisely communicate how her abilities and teaching skills were applicable and beneficial to the workplace. At first, Pat was hesitant to twist her experience in this fashion, but when I pointed out how valuable these skills would be to any traditional workplace, she gained the confidence to speak about her gifts to potential employers.

FROM TEACHER TO ASSISTANT DIRECTOR

Shortly after our coaching sessions, Pat was offered the position of Education Director of the East End Art Council in Riverhead, NY, and she immediately accepted! The Council is a nonprofit organization that supports local artists. From the beginning, Pat put her mark on the organization: membership and event attendance and frequency soared under her reign. She is credited with the expansion of the EEAC Community School of the Arts, and she initiated the Riverhead Community Mosaic: Street Painting Festival to bring attention to the school and to raise scholarship funds for needy students. As she had when she was a child in her family, Pat began to establish herself as a leader in the organization and have a profound influence on her environment. She developed new programs for the Council to offer its artist members and the

Lipstick Leadership

"I learned an important lesson from my Aunt Evelyn, a farm wife. When I was young, I used to think that Evelyn was the most patient person I had ever met. Evelyn was slow to judge and quick to understand. She taught me that you never know what is happening with a person until you ask. This has helped me to forge business relationships that I would otherwise never have considered."

~ Julie Viskup, Law Professor at Champlain College

**Submit your best "Mom's Wisdom" story at
www.LipstickLeadership.com today!**

community by tapping into her creativity and her ability to build collaborative events. She perfected the art of leveraging the talents of committee members and the board of directors, getting everyone involved in the events and workings of the Council. In 1999, Pat was awarded the honor of News-Review "Educator of the Year."

When Pat recognized the artists of the Council lacked the business skills to sell their art, she organized a seminar for them and asked me to teach a course on marketing for artists. Afterwards, many of the struggling artists in the audience flocked around Pat and I to thank us for providing them with the tools and tactics to get their work seen and sold. Once again, Pat utilized her gift of knowing how to ask for involvement in such a way that people automatically want to give of their time, treasure and talent — a great skill for an advocate of a non-profit organization to have!

MOVING UP IN THE COUNCIL

When the position of Executive Director of the Council opened up in 2000, Pat moved confidently toward this amazing opportunity. Remembering all we had discussed during our coaching sessions, she entered into the application stage knowing she could out deliver any other candidate for the job.

Pat has been the Executive Director for over seven years now, bringing her leadership into the forefront and raising the Council to greater levels of success than it has ever known. She and her staff and Board of Directors have added many amazing programs, including The Teeny Awards, a high school theatre arts recognition program; Canvassing Riverhead, a joint effort with the Riverhead Chamber of Commerce; Secret Garden, the annual EEAC fundraiser; and CONTACT!, a downtown initiative that encourages visitors to Riverhead businesses during school vacation weeks. As the official leader of the EEAC, Pat has doubled membership to the Arts Council, expanded the Council's reach in the community, and initiated the renovation of the Carriage House to provide artists with ample studio space. Through all of her accomplishments, it was her skill at knowing how to lead from within that brought her the success she richly deserves. And I'm not the only one who recognizes what an amazing woman Pat is: she was voted Woman of the Year by the East End Women's Network!

MBA (Mom's Business Acumen) Class: Cultivating Power Contacts and Connections

Having a powerful advocate in your organization helps to promote your ideas, career and projects, paving the way for effecting change from within an organization. But how do you get someone who has the authority to lead to back your ideas? Here are some ways to develop relationships with the players in your organization, giving you the opportunity to leverage your time with influential people:

1. Make a list of everyone you would like to know, and more importantly, to have know YOU! This is your wish list. Once it is identified, you can get to work. Remember this is a wish, so dream big!

2. Do your research to find the contact information for each of these people.

3. Get to know and befriend their assistants. They are the gatekeepers who can make or break the possibility of getting ten minutes with a busy person.

4. Contact them for a 15-minute interview for your company newsletter.

5. Find out what charitable boards they serve on and volunteer.

6. Find out where they work-out in the morning, and get your exercise gear on!

7. Have your 30-second elevator speech ready just in case you find them on the elevator!

8. Make your calls for requests for meetings early in the morning, 7-8 a.m., or in the evening, 5-7 p.m. The gate-keeper has usually gone home, but the boss is still there picking up their own phone.

It is all about being in the right place at the right time…and seizing the opportunity to connect! Don't use your level in your organization as an excuse — go out and meet some influential people today and start the process of your own development as a leader!!

CHAPTER 8

IT'S JUST FINE

SKIING WITH MIMI

When I was in ninth grade, my parents bought a twenty-foot Winnebago motor home for the seven of us to travel in and see the country. Mimi and Pop-Pop believed in investing in us as people by providing us with experiences that would build character and develop our personalities. Both of my parents were teachers, so we had the opportunity to have long stretches of time where they were available to take trips. One of our favorite family activities was skiing. My parents would load all five of us kids into the Winnie with all of our equipment and make the eight-hour drive upstate to the mountains. We would park in the mountain lot by the base lodge and use the Winnie as our home where we would eat, sleep and dress during the trip.

We were a working middle class family with only a small amount of disposable income. These ski trips were a considerable commitment of time and money so no matter what the weather was, we took full advantage of our vacation and we skied. We skied in sunshine, snow storms, hail storms and even in the rain. When the skies opened up and it poured, my mother would get some resistance from her brood of teenagers. "But Mom, we can't ski in the *rain*!" we would protest, and she would reply, "It's just fine. Here's a garbage bag to go over your ski gear. Poke your head and arms through; it'll keep you dry and we'll have a perfect day of skiing." Then she would invariably treat us to one of her poems:

> *"Whether the weather is good, or whether the*
> *weather is not, we'll weather the weather whatever*
> *the weather — whether we like it or not!"*

Mom's positive attitude that everything in her world is "just fine" and her weather poem — not to mention her proclivity to break out into song from time to time — are legendary in my house. To this day, her grandchildren often quote her in times of adversity and certainly in times of foul weather.

THE FIVE-SECOND RULE

I remember one such trip during ski season when we drove to Lake Placid, NY, about ten hours from home. We pulled into the campground and staked out our site. My father parked the Winnie and proceeded to get hooked up to water and electric while the children raced to the top of the mountain to ski.

Later on when the skiing for the day was done, we gathered in the Winnie while Mimi began pulling together dinner. She had made a big pot of lentil soup at home and thought we could eat it all weekend. We were all starving after a full day of skiing and a hearty warm soup sounded like heaven to our frozen ears! Mimi had just set the pot on the little propane stove when the camper suddenly started to lurch to one side and rocked back to the other. The soup went flying into the air and landed all over the olive green shag carpet!

My father had his back to the mess and walked out the door without noticing dinner on the floor. He called out, "I'm going to level us out," and went to work on fixing the camper. My mother was silent, her eyes darting from the pile of cold soup to where my father stood outside the window to the wide eyes of her five children. After a moment, she sprang into action. To our shock, she started scooping up the soup from the top of the puddle and put it back into the pot! As she spooned up the broth and lentils, she suddenly became aware of all of our eyes and quietly turned to us and said, "It's just fine. Shh! I'm just taking from the top; that part never touched the carpet. It's just fine. Shh! Don't tell Dad!" Mom ladled enough soup to fill our seven mouths and then scrubbed the carpet clean before my father returned to the camper. Although none of us kids were very enthusiastic about eating lentil soup (with just a dash of olive green shag carpeting), we ate quietly during dinner, trying not to laugh as our father complimented the chef!

MORE LIVING TO DO

In my Aunt Ruthie, I found another great role-model for maintaining a positive attitude. Ruthie was not a blood aunt; she was a sorority sister of my mother's. When my parents graduated from college, there was a lot of growth on Long Island. New communities were developing, resulting in more homes being built, families moving in, and children needing schooling. This led to a tremendous need for teachers in the new school districts that were popping up all over. About twenty of my parents close college friends — all brand new teachers — moved out to Long Island for new jobs, creating a community of their own. They became my "aunts" and "uncles" and I loved them dearly, but it was Aunt Ruthie who impacted my life dramatically.

Aunt Ruthie and my Uncle David had five kids whose ages paralleled the kids in my family perfectly. When I was in the sixth grade, Aunt Ruthie had a stroke and a series of open-heart surgeries. The doctors predicted she would not survive, but they didn't know my Aunt Ruthie. She had fight in her and she was not ready to let go. When the doctors told her she would never walk again, she refused to accept life confined to a wheel-chair even though she was paralyzed on one side. Aunt Ruthie always said she had more living to do, and so she worked hard toward rehabilitating herself and walking again one day.

Lipstick Leadership

"My husband's grandmother, 'Nana Vi,' redecorated her apartment at age 92! Her sense of optimism was her greatest gift to me. With a book about to be published and an associated business plan in the works, optimism is what has helped me deal with the challenges along the way. Coming from a family of worriers, I had to learn to be optimistic, and Nana Vi's example was my guide."

~ Carol Fishman Cohen, Co-Author of "Back on the Career Track"

Advance your career with the help of Michelle's FREE e-zine. Sign up today at www.LipstickLeadership.com!

The amazing thing about Aunt Ruthie was not so much that she lived past her doctor's expectations, but her approach to *how* she lived. As far as she was concerned, she was just fine. No disability was going to get in her way. She wanted to continue to be the active woman she was as a physical education teacher before the stroke. So when her whole group of friends bought boats to live on at the beach, she and Uncle David did, too. Aunt Ruthie lived on a boat, graduating from a wheelchair to a cane because of her determination and the positive attitude she chose to adopt in the face of her adversity. Uncle David would carry her off the back of the boat onto the dock, and she would make her way up to the overlook so she could see us all swimming in the ocean. She continued doing the things she loved, like paying bridge with the girls, and refused to let her physical ailments get in the way.

Aunt Ruthie was an independent, proud and classy woman who chose to engage in life in a positive way despite physical limitations that could have defeated her. No matter how broken down her body was, Ruthie was "just fine" as far as she was concerned. When I was a freshman in college, Aunt Ruthie caught pneumonia and passed away. I will always remember her as a woman who had the strength and attitude to make a remarkable impression on anyone she met.

Simple Truth from Mom:
If you believe it's just fine...it is!
You create your own reality

The most powerful lesson I learned from Mimi and Aunt Ruthie is to take responsibility for my reality. In life and in work things don't always go as planned, but that's no reason to give up or pass the blame onto someone else. If you take responsibility for having a positive attitude and developing a strategic solution to any problem that arises, you'll be amazed at the unbelievable reality you're able to create.

A BIG DECISION

When I first made the decision to start my own business, I examined where my life was at the time, the skills and talents I had in my personal arsenal, and how I might translate that into revenue if I ventured out on my own into the business world. At that point, I split my time between being a stay-at-home mom to my two sons, four- and five-year-olds (who are now nineteen and twenty-year-olds!), and a teacher of business courses in the evening at the local college. I had recently been asked by the dean at the college to speak at a few local business conferences and that event yielded my first coaching clients, spurring the idea to start my own business. But when I started to give it some thought, my initial excitement was tempered with doubts and questions: *could I successfully make the transition to being an entrepreneur?*

THE BUMPY FLIGHT

During the winter semester break, I had the unusual luxury of flying from my home in upstate New York to Florida to visit my parents without the company of my husband and my little urchins. As the flight took off and I settled into my seat for the seven hour journey, I began seriously contemplating the move from teaching to launching my new business.

An hour into the flight, the plane started lurching and pitching. The helpful flight attendant explained we were experiencing turbulence, and I relaxed a little in my seat. Flying is not my favorite hobby, but a few bumps were nothing compared to rappelling down the side of a building, right? Then I noticed the man sitting next to me was visibly rattled by this change in our flight conditions. He must not have had a mom like Mimi or he would have known *it was just fine!* I struck up a conversation with him in the hope of calming him down a bit. He introduced himself as Ramon, and he explained he had just concluded some business in New York — he worked in the field of Human Resources — and was heading back home to Boca Raton. I kept him talking about his business, peppering him with questions to try and take his mind off the flight, and it was working beautifully...until the plane took a deep swoop down and then leveled out.

NETWORKING AT 30,000 FEET

Ramon was pale and shaking, so I pushed the flight attendant button. When she arrived, I ordered myself a drink and asked Ramon if he wanted one. "Yes!" he exclaimed right away. I paid for our drinks, and after a few sips, Ramon seemed to calm down. He thanked me for my graciousness, and we chatted a bit. I decided to take the plunge and tell him about my consulting business — he didn't know it only existed in my head for now! I talked about the type of training and coaching services I offered, and he seemed very interested.

Lipstick Leadership

"My mother's courage, strength, resourcefulness and unconditional love shaped my self-image which allowed me to pursue everything and anything I have ever wanted to achieve in my life. Her actions taught me

to persevere even in adversity and to believe anything is possible for me. Although she was not born in this country, she has amazed me with her ability to reinvent herself many times over! Not only does she have spirit but it is all grounded with an incredible faith that she has also instilled in me. My mother is my role model...she has led her life with the utmost grace and soul. I have grown to become a resilient woman who has approached all of my work with passion and the belief in my ability to achieve all of my goals. Because of the solid foundation she created for me, I don't hesitate to 'go for it' within my work every day. I'm not afraid to try new things, welcome challenges and have the confidence to plow right through them."

~ Rita Allen, Rita B. Allen Associates

Submit your best "Mom's Wisdom" story at www.LipstickLeadership.com today!

At the end of the trip as we were approaching the runway, Ramon thanked me once again for helping him through this rollercoaster of a flight, and he asked for my business card. I recognized this as the first step toward making my entrepreneurial vision a reality! And I didn't have a card to give him! So I told a tiny fib and said this was a trip for pleasure and I left all remnants of work back at my office. He asked me to send him a brochure on my business and remarked offhandedly the company he worked for might need someone with my expertise. "Maybe you've heard of us?" I could barely contain myself — of course I had! This corporation, with its 26 subsidiary companies, was HUGE!

CORPORATE CLIENT #1

When I arrived back in Connecticut after my vacation, I immediately designed business cards, a brochure and a website for my new company, Saxton Consulting. Within days, I sent Ramon a package of information and prayed for the best. Months passed and I didn't hear from him, but I didn't lose hope. I was proud I had taken the risk, and besides, I was too busy getting my new company off the ground!

Out of the blue I got a call from the CIO of Ramon's employer. He had been forwarded my brochure with a glowing recommendation from their corporate office, and he was looking for someone to train the CIOs from all 26 subsidiaries! The CIOs were scheduled to present a new IT initiative to the boards of directors for each of the subsidiaries, and apparently, communication was not their strong suit. Would I be willing to fly down to New Jersey, meet with CIOs from around the world, and provide them with a week of extensive coaching? I accepted faster than Ramon said yes to that drink on the flight!

This event was my first big corporate assignment, and it was a rousing success that led to even greater things for my company…and it happened because I projected who and what I wanted to become into the universe. I was open to a potential opportunity and I took action, and in doing so, I also took control of my own future, went out on a limb, and committed to my own future reality as if it already existed.

MBA (Mom's Business Acumen) Class: Choosing Your Reality

We as a society make a lot of excuses for why our career, lives and relationships don't work. In this chapter's MBA class, however, you don't get a list...you get a sermon. I'm preaching on Mimi's behalf because your reality is "just fine" if that's what you choose to make it!

If you want a perfect example of the old saying, "Misery loves company," you need to look no further than most workplace break rooms today. With few exceptions, there is at least one person in every organization who complains, complains, and complains. Their boss is unfair; the workload is too heavy; the benefits and pay aren't good enough; they don't have a nice enough office; so-and-so didn't deserve that raise...and so on.

This malcontent spreads his or her negativity like germs in a nursery school. They lie in wait in the break room, ready to pounce on unsuspecting employees who come in for a cup of coffee or a donut; instead, they get an earful of just how awful it is to work for this company. Unfortunately, this kind of negativity is a powerful thing. Before long, the malcontent army has grown, and they become the majority, poisoning the workplace environment with their dissatisfaction.

So what do you do if you're an employee who finds satisfaction in your work, who agrees with the policies and procedures of the company, who has a positive outlook and who actually likes your job?

It can be lonely out there for a satisfied worker, and as someone who loves what they do for a living, I want to reach out to those who are happy with their careers — and living among those who aren't — and offer my advice on how to maintain a positive attitude in a negative work environment.

It's no big secret that some people are truly working just to receive a paycheck. They're only interested in getting what they can out of the company versus giving anything back. While it's true some companies take, take, take from their employees and give them the heave-ho without any regard to their service and loyalty, I challenge you to find a company that rewards hard work and loyalty — there are plenty of them out there. Good employers see the value their employees are providing, and they are doing everything they can to hold onto talented individuals. Do your research!

If you've already found a company you want to grow with and your stuck among a group of co-workers who grumble through their days, the first thing you should remind yourself when you start to get pulled into their grousing is that your boss is probably really pleased with your positive attitude. He or she has recognized your sincere excitement over your work, and he or she will reward you for it and help you foster it. So schedule a time to talk with him or her about upcoming projects, goals that have been met, innovations and new challenges on the horizon. You'll find a little pep talk with someone who is as committed to the company as you are can really boost your mood.

But while your boss may encourage your passion, your co-workers may feel a little intimidated by it. People are often skittish around passionate people because they don't quite understand where that passion is coming from — and people fear what they don't understand. Remember this and be sure you don't push your own perspective onto someone else. Just focus on your own exhilaration and feel good about the fact that you're contributing in a positive way to your company. Perhaps your passion for work will subtly rub off on your

Lipstick Leadership

"My mom was a single parent, a workaholic mom who worked three jobs to put food on the table for my sister and me. This has given me a boundless well of strength. Whenever I feel like complaining because I am tired due to a long filming schedule, I think of my mom who worked for longer hours for more primal reasons...feeding her daughters. When I feel my weakest, I call my mother to be with me emotionally and spiritually. She has helped shape me into a woman who knows that my opportunities are limitless if I am willing to work hard."

~ Shalini Kantayya, Activist/Film Director,
   www.ADropofLife.com

**Advance your career with the help of
Michelle's FREE e-zine. Sign up today at
www.LipstickLeadership.com!**

co-workers. Enthusiasm can be just as contagious as negativity, but remember, real change — especially a shift in corporate culture — can take time, so don't be disappointed if you're the only one clapping after an announcement of a new project.

Try to find someone else in your organization that is equally happy with their career. Having someone you can share good work news with and go to for a mental boost during the workday can really help you maintain that positive attitude. Keep the level of engagement to a minimum with the griping group as well. Take on projects that are challenging and that keep you busy so you won't have a lot of extra time for the negative coffee talk going on.

Know that most people who are very unhappy at work are usually pretty insecure about the type of work they're doing. Your positive attitude may have your co-workers feeling a little bit unsure about your motives. Some may feel like you're trying to make the rest of the team look bad. In that case, your best defense is good communication. Let your co-workers know you're passionate about your work and excited to be doing what you're doing. Explain that there is no hidden agenda and point out that if they can't muster up any sort of positive attitude about their job, maybe it's time they evaluate their own happiness and figure out what kind of work will make them just as passionate as you are.

Personally, I love to start my day with affirmations, positive statements that project what I want to have happen in my day, and a clear picture of what I want my day to look like. And then no matter what anyone else says or does, I have those affirmations and daily plan to think about, and I can recall them and give myself an instant shot of positive vibes.

Remember, at the end of the day, it's about how YOU feel about your career, not what someone else thinks. YOU have to feel good about the type of work you're doing, and you have the right to remain positive!

Can I get an AMEN?

So what project or circumstance are YOU complaining about? Take control of that problem and focus on possible solutions. Don't judge the likelihood of success: just get creative and think BIG. Make your reality a better one today!

CHAPTER 9

WHO ARE YOU TALKING TO?

GETTING TO KNOW YOU...GETTING TO KNOW ALL ABOUT YOU...

I am the mother of two boys, now nineteen and twenty-years-old, and there could not be two siblings who are more different. The boys are a reflection of how different my husband and I are. We have very different ways of executing both work and play, and though we see the world differently, our overall vision of success and what we want out of life is in line with each other (which probably explains how we've stayed married for twenty-one years!). Because of our differing personalities, communicating with each of us requires completely different styles and tactics.

After our sons were born and they started to develop their own personalities, we noticed how similar Kevin is to me and Michael is to Rich. We realized that the key to communicating effectively with them (and getting them to do what we wanted!) was to closely examine how we learned to communicate with each other based on our personality styles.

So who exactly are Michelle and Rich Drake?

MICHELLE, THE ARTIST

I am a strange mix of "the creative type" and a strategist and communicator who sees the overall "big picture." I excel in my profession as communication strategist because it's people-oriented and usually right out there, front and center. But I also love creating something out of nothing; it's the artist in me, and my medium of choice is painting. When my son Michael moved out of the house to attend college in Florida last year, I waited an acceptable amount of time…and then turned his bedroom into my own personal art studio!

My studio is my "happy place" where everything makes sense to me, where I feel comfortable with who I am and what I'm all about, where I can focus on myself and my place in the world. As a professional speaker, I make my living with words. My paintings pick up where the words leave off, expressing things to which words cannot do justice. My early work was pretty basic and predictable, mostly because I think I hadn't found the way into my own personal artistic expression. I struggled to try and fit in with a traditional artistic process and its outcome. I tried to paint what I saw, not what I felt. It wasn't until I made a shift in *how* I paint that my art began to reflect my personal take on the world going on around me and inside me. For me, art has become painting the inspiration of what I see, allowing myself to interpret what I see and translating that into the art I produce using my hands instead of a brush to paint.

Three years ago, I met an artist named Michelle Bellici. She really changed my life creatively. She taught me a technique of painting that was all about getting in touch with what I was feeling. In the past, I painted things I was familiar with, and my art reflected my surroundings but not necessarily who I am. I painted beach scenes, my children, seascapes and boats. Michelle taught me to get in touch with my materials by painting with my hands in order to let art emerge from within me instead of capturing what I was seeing outside me. I began to express my feelings through color and textures. Once I learned this technique, it felt as though I had always painted this way. I had finally become a true artist.

If you'd like to enjoy some of my art, visit:
www.ArtistMichelleDrake.com
and don't forget to claim my gift to YOU…a FREE
set of "Michelle's Favorite Paintings" postcards!

RICH, THE PROCESS GUY

At The Cove Group, Inc., my husband and business partner, Rich, is a direct contrast to my creative and intuitive style. With his background in mechanical engineering, he brings the tactics and support to our business. He is very organized, methodical and process-oriented; I might have a brilliant idea or strategy and a general idea of where it needs to go, but Rich will know how to organize all of the details to execute the hundred little tasks that need to be done in order to have success.

Rich's "happy place" is the garage. His neat and tidy garage is very different from my chaotic art studio. Many clients have been quite intrigued by the amazing cars he's built and have asked to visit his garage to look at the result of all of his work. He has built a Factory Five Cobra and is presently working on a Lotus. He builds these cars from nothing more than boxes of wires and metal scraps that were stripped out of old automobiles. For creating these automotive "works of art," Rich has a very different process than mine, and his is very organized and linear.

When you enter his garage, the first thing you might notice is the lack of clutter. There is one project in the center of the garage and a variety of labeled canisters and cabinets lining the walls. There is probably also an old junk car, or "donor" car where Rich scavenges parts from as he builds. As he strips the donor car of useable parts, he cleans and labels each part and immediately puts it in the appropriate cabinet. When the time comes to use those parts in the new car, he knows exactly where they are and how they go together.

Lipstick Leadership

"...my mother taught me to be an effective communicator. She has the ability to gain trust from an initial meeting. My mother is the best at meeting someone and gaining their trust immediately. In a world where sales are everything, trust is the key factor to success, especially for a banker. It makes people take the extra step to doing business with you rather than your competition. [My mother] also has a unique skill of getting people to want to be around her, and [she] can make them smile... [People] are very open, honest and feel comfortable giving her information about their needs. In business, this translates to knowing enough information about a customer or prospect to figure out products and services to help them. If not for my mom, I would not be where I am today..."

~ June Goguen, Vice President of the Commercial Lending Division, Eastern Bank

Submit your best "Mom's Wisdom" story at www.LipstickLeadership.com today!

For Rich, there is beauty and peace in carefully tearing something down so he can methodically put it back together. His process is more about connecting the pieces in the way they need to go to work effectively than being chaotically creative like my process. At the end of his sessions in the garage, he puts everything back in its place, every tool, every piece of equipment, and every part so when he goes into his garage the next day, he is starting with a blank slate. His key to success is starting clean and uncluttered to be able to be creative. Rich likes symmetry; for him, symmetry makes it easy for him to create the path for systems, processes and tactics to bring a project or organization to a successful outcome.

THE ARTIST AND THE PROCESS GUY AT WORK

When we're at work, Rich and I often work together in creating a new project or resolving an issue. Rich will observe how I plan and develop, and he creates the system to be able to deliver the project and then replicate the outcome for another client. He is our timeline person and manages all of the support work behind my creative efforts. With all of my books, my radio show, all the audio and video products, the speaking engagements and the coaching and entrepreneurial programs, there has to be a solid support system. There has to be a team that executes on all the tasks pertaining to the ideas that get generated. With the help of my amazing project manager Rachel — who is cut from the same cloth as Rich — Rich is in charge of developing and executing those processes. He is the person who brings order and clarity into our business. Armed with flowcharts for every single project we are executing, Rich keeps everyone on task and everything running smoothly forward so we understand exactly what needs to be done, who needs to be doing it, and what the deadlines are.

For years, Rich saw solutions as black-and-white...then he met me. I saw solutions in hot pink! And after twenty-one years of marriage and seven years of being in business together, he has gotten comfortable with the "colors" of my world, and I've gotten comfortable with the definite plans of his.

POLAR OPPOSITES

The combination of my creative and analytical mind with Rich's organized and tactical mind is extremely powerful for us in business and at home. It's no big surprise that two people who are so different might produce children who are equally different from each other. Our two sons reflect each of our personalities, aptitudes and approaches to life in general. From a parenting perspective, this created a situation where Mom and Dad needed to handle each of them quite differently. We needed to understand their different communication styles and speak to each within their respective styles in order to be able to get the desired outcome.

My oldest son Michael is now in college studying mechanical engineering, just like his father. Like Rich, he likes things in a very particular way, and when he gets something into his head, it's very difficult to change his mind. Michael is headstrong, passionate, driven, disciplined, and a hard worker. He sees the impact of what he is doing today on where his future is heading. He has clear goals and sometimes an obsessive personality. As Michael is growing into the man he was born to be, he is learning to control his emotions, but as a child, that was something he really struggled with. When he was angry or upset or even happy

Lipstick Leadership

"Because my sister has cerebral palsy, I spent my child-hood watching my mother speak up at hospitals, doctors' offices, and various other settings to get the attention or assistance my sister needed. This provided an excellent role model for me to ask for what I need rather than always meekly going along with things."

~ Rochelle Kopp, Author of "The Rice-Paper Ceiling"

Advance your career with the help of Michelle's FREE e-zine. Sign up today at www.LipstickLeadership.com!

and joyous, he couldn't hide it. In communicating with Michael, I always needed to be very direct and to the point.

My son Kevin is pretty much the polar opposite. Kevin is very people-oriented, a proverbial "social butterfly." He runs with a big pack of friends who adore his carefree nature and easy-going attitude. He thinks about the moment and lives in the moment with little regard to the impact his actions and decisions may have on the future. Planning for the future? Not Kevin! He would rather live day-by-day than structure his life into neat increments. He's currently studying business in college and enjoying a social life almost as hectic as his class schedule!

Even the boys' summer jobs reflect the differences in their personalities. Kevin enjoys his summer job as a waiter because he gets to spend his days surfing and then gets to interact with people all evening. His winter job as a salesperson in a sporting goods store is also perfect because, again, he gets to interact with people (and get free trips to the mountain to snowboard!). Michael works as an assistant mechanic in a garage where he can focus on the intricacies of cars (just like his father) and utilize his engineering talents to get engines running again.

BOATING WITH THE BOYS

Managing these boys required two different approaches no matter what the task. When we relocated to Connecticut, we were blessed to find a home in a beautiful little community called Lord's Point which overlooks Fisher's Island Sound. Northeast sailors know Fisher's Island Sound as one of the more treacherous bodies of water for boating. It is clear, beautiful and well-protected but littered with reefs, shoals and rocks lying just below the surface. Learning to operate a boat safely in that environment takes time. You must study the charts and find the marker buoys and landmarks to acclimate yourself to the waters. We bought a boat the second year we were in Connecticut and started the process of learning to stay out of trouble.

The boys, of course, were not ones to just sit in the boat and go for a ride; they insisted on operating the boat themselves. Not only did they need to learn to operate the boat correctly, they had to do it in a location where a wrong turn can be very dangerous. Rich set out to devise a training course and qualification test for the boys so we didn't have to anxiously stand by the water with binoculars any time they were out in the boat. The trick would be to teach them in such a way that the information would stick with both of them, leaving nothing to chance. Rich soon realized making it stick meant teaching them individually, each in a way that suited their aptitudes and motivations.

Michael, the mechanical engineer, quickly picked up starting, operating and maneuvering the boat. With intense focus, he figured out the charts and the global positioning system (GPS) and pointed out where all the danger spots were. He methodically developed a picture of each area to avoid and found the markers he would use to alert him when he might be too close. Michael was taught how to navigate home if fog closed in or if he was out at night. He was motivated to learn everything, every last detail up and down the New England coast so he would not be limited in when or where he could take the boat. Accordingly, he had to develop advanced skills and knowledge to meet his objective.

Kevin simply wanted to use the boat to get to the beach and the surfing hot spots so he didn't have to drive his car, deal with summer traffic and struggle to find a place to park. Kevin was a more typical teenager. While he is blessed with many amazing traits, mechanical aptitude is not the strongest among them. He required a more detailed education on the mechanical operation of the boat than did Michael. Priming the fuel, using the choke, setting the trim and operating the GPS took a bit more time for Kevin to master. On the water, Kevin excelled. His visual ability meant we could travel a route, point out the obstacles and Kevin could then keep this image in his head. He proved this later on by successfully navigating home after the fog rolled in and the GPS simultaneously quit. Because his goal was one route, he learned it well but was restricted on where he could go.

Learning how to address the different personalities of our boys was easy because Rich and I had years of practice communicating with each other! We learned quickly that if we were going to be successful parents to Michael and Kevin, we would need to remember who we were talking to and how to get through to them in the best way possible.

Simple Truth from Mom:
Know who you're talking to and ADJUST!

When managing a business or a department, you need to be able to adapt your communication style to fit the type of person you're dealing with. Maximum results come from professionals who understand this concept and can adapt their message without

> compromising who they are or the information they're delivering. This is especially beneficial in an interview setting: understanding how someone best receives information can make or break your ability to get the job, make the sale, motivate the team or meet the department goals.

MARKETING YOU!

For several years, I've been working with an executive, Diana, on creating and executing communication strategies for her department's marketing campaigns. During one of our sessions, she approached me with a more personal assignment: she asked if I could coach her on how to "market" herself professionally. A position three levels up in her organization had been recently vacated, and she was planning on putting her name into the running. Diana knew it was a long shot, but she felt like she had nothing to lose in going for it. She wanted to use the same marketing strategy I had developed for her department and adapt it to suit her bid for this new position.

We began by gathering data on the job itself, picking apart the posting, the job description and the preferred qualifications. I revealed to her the secret to reading between the lines of job postings, and she was amazed at all the useful pieces of info we amassed. Next, we tailored her resume to focus on the main deliverables this job would require. She had the skills and the experience; all we needed to do was use the terminology and repackage the data so her résumé projected her as the perfect fit for the job.

Finally, we took a look at some of the internal reports we developed over the past few years to highlight what her department had accomplished, and we re-created them to highlight what *Diana* had accomplished. These sales brochures were the perfect way to demonstrate her skill, leadership and ability to cultivate a high-performance team.

Diana submitted the materials we developed, and we both waited with our fingers crossed.

THE PANEL INTERVIEW

Diana called me a few days later and jubilantly told me she had passed the first round with flying colors. Based on her tailored written submission, she had wowed the committee enough to make it through to round two: a panel interview with a ten-minute presentation followed by an intensive question and answer period. Needless to say, after her initial excitement wore off, she became really nervous about this portion of the process.

We started preparing for the interview and presentation by breaking her coaching sessions into seven categories:

1. Analyze competition

2. Analyze interview panel

3. Execution plan, a.k.a. the "100 Days Plan"

4. Slide show

5. Handouts

6. Questions and answers

7. PRACTICE!

ANALYZING THE COMPETITION

The first session she and I had together consisted of understanding how she measured up to her competition. Since this was an internal posting for a job, Diana had the advantage of doing a little digging around the office, and she was able to find out who else got an invitation to present to the interview panel. We did a SWOT analysis on each candidate — including Diana — and compared each element side-by-side.

Good news! We found Diana's strengths far out numbered her weaknesses within her own SWOT analysis, and in comparison to the other candidates, she annihilated them! Now it was just up to us to create a compelling presentation that would not only prove why she should jump three levels in the organization but also carefully (and tactfully) display her strengths in light of her competitions' weaknesses.

ANALYZING THE INTERVIEW PANEL

Our next session focused on the most important part: determining who was on the interview panel and how Diana could package her message to appeal to each and every member. This information would guide us through all of the other preparation we needed to do.

Diana discovered her interview panel consisted of:

- ◆ A human resources representative
- ◆ A scientist who would be her customer
- ◆ A global team member who would be a peer
- ◆ A sales manager who would be a subordinate
- ◆ A site head who would be her boss

It was quite a diverse group, and we knew it would be difficult to meet everyone's issues and concerns, but we were ready to meet the challenge head-on. After identifying who was going to be making the decision about hiring, we needed to know *how* they each processed information and *what* they each felt was the most important quality/experience the perfect candidate would have to possess. We needed to be clear in how we "framed" Diana in the interview process, so we broke down each of the personalities represented.

Lipstick Leadership

"My mother taught me to 'catch more flies with honey than with vinegar!' I try to remember this when I am about to scream at someone for not doing what I want, when I want it!"

~ Carole Lieberman, M.D., Beverly Hills psychiatrist/ author/talk show host

Submit your best "Mom's Wisdom" story at www.LipstickLeadership.com today!

Diana had successful dealings with **the human resource representative** in the past. She knew he valued his relationships with people, but he also liked clear procedures and for people to follow those specific procedures. So when she spoke about her abilities in those areas, I coached Diana to make sure that she made eye contact with the HR representative and that she noted her ability to follow the rules and cite specific examples of her doing so in relation to her experience.

The scientist, who would be her customer if she landed this job, was a complete mystery to Diana. She hadn't been able to find out any information about her, and she had never had any interaction with this person in the past. Luckily for Diana, she had made many friends working at her company for the last seven years, and she was able to ask around and find out from her peers what her potential scientific customer was all about. Diana discovered the scientist was a woman who was very detail-oriented, known to be a little bit abrupt, and preferred people who get to the point quickly. She liked "just the facts," statements uncluttered by emotion. We knew in Diana's presentation, we needed to be able to quantify her accomplishments and reasons why she should be selected. Diana would need to bring statistics illustrating her positive impact on the company, and she would also need to be able to reassure this scientist she was going to analyze the customer needs and make sure she was delivering to them...all while being very concise and to-the-point.

The global team member would become one of Diana's peers, someone she would need to work with if she got the job. Finding out about this person was important both for this selection process and for her future in this position. The global team member focused more on concept and vision rather than execution and tactics — a creative type who always had great ideas but didn't always execute on those ideas effectively. We needed to make sure Diana was able to demonstrate her ability to see "the big picture" as well as her skill in executing the details — a complement to the vision of the global team member. Creating a clear execution plan that was in line with the existing vision of the group ended up being very important because it demonstrated Diana's ability to collaborate, a critical point for the global team member. Diana needed to balance the line between speaking confidently about herself and speak in terms of what she could accomplish as part of a team.

The sales manager was a classic embodiment of the "salesperson" stereotype. He was very personable, talkative and likeable, and had a short attention span that would be a challenge for Diana. He was accustomed to putting people together and then moving on to the next thing. As a manager, he had risen through the ranks of the organization and would be an ally in Diana's own rise to the top, so she needed to get short, vital bits of information out before she lost his attention. We would need to make sure her slide show and handouts would work well as a neatly packaged variety of information that stimulated his preference for seeing pieces of information rather than listening to a whole lot of information.

The last person on this interview panel was **the site head**, the woman who would become her boss. The site head was actually the person who gave Diana the heads-up about the position and encouraged her to apply. She was also an advocate for Diana because they both served on a few of the same philanthropic committees; they both knew how the other worked and communicated. The site head was a no-nonsense, execution-oriented person who was very passionate about giving back to the community. Because Diana had sat on those philanthropic boards with her potential future boss, it certainly gave her a bit of an advantage.

THE LAST STEPS

After we knew her competition and who she would be presenting to on the interview panel, we focused our attention on her presentation: her "100 Day Plan," the slideshow and handouts, and preparation for the Q&A session.

The "100 Day Plan" is your plan for the first hundred days in your new position. It's a strategic map for you to follow as you start a new job, and it's also an impressive way to convince the hiring panel that not only are you committed to bringing great success to the position, you know exactly what your goals and objectives are for those first few months. With it, you've got a plan of attack already in place! With my help, Diana drafted her "100 Day Plan" and she was ready to walk into that panel confident in her ability to hit the ground running if they gave her the opportunity to do so.

Next, we worked on her slideshow and handouts. At the mention of PowerPoint, Diana groaned. "I hate sitting through those endless slides!" she said, and I explained I had only three slides in mind. She was elated but doubtful we could hit all the major points she needed to on just a few slides. I worked with her on honing her message — "What's in it for them?" I repeated again and again — and in the end, she had her major talking points right there on those slides with nary an extraneous word in sight!

Then we worked on a handout to leave behind after the interview was over. Most candidates would leave behind their résumé, but I wanted her to really stand out from the crowd. We developed a "one sheet," a document popular with professional speakers. A one sheet is exactly that: a single sheet that briefly outlines all of the important information about the speaker, or in this case, about Diana the job candidate. We crafted a handout that contained the major points of her background, job experience, and accomplishments (including statistics). This handout would become an even more powerful "sales brochure" than her résumé.

With the materials of her presentation in the bag, we turned our focus to prepping for her speech and her question and answer session. I gave Diana my best tips for projecting confidence (even if her palms were sweating!) and how to overcome nervous habits to present a message that was clear and concise. After the initial run-through, I made adjustments to how she would deliver her presentation, and she ran through it again. And again. And again. We worked on "#7: PRACTICE!" for several sessions! She practiced and we even role played. I put myself in the position of each member of her hiring panel and came up with the type of questions I thought they would logically ask. I coached Diana through the toughest questions I could think of, and by the time her interview rolled around, she could have done it in her sleep!

When the day of her interview arrived, I spoke to Diana beforehand to offer my last minute support. She was surprisingly calm and collected, and when I questioned her stress-free status, she laughed and replied, "You've coached me so well that I know no matter what the outcome is, I've done everything in my power to present a compelling and accurate case for awarding me the

Lipstick Leadership

"When I was a little girl, my mother told me that women are like an iron fist in a velvet glove...which meant that we don't have to speak loud, shout, or be rude...we just have to be solid and strong on the inside to get things done. My mother, very softly and sweetly, never takes NO for an answer. As a filmmaker, I need a lot of people to help me get a story told. The ability to speak sweetly and appreciatively while still getting my ideas across with authority has been an advantage in making films that make a social statement...thank you mom!"

~ Shalini Kantayya, Activist/Film Director,
   www.ADropofLife.com

**Advance your career with the help of
Michelle's FREE e-zine. Sign up today at
www.LipstickLeadership.com!**

position. What's there to worry about?" Diana knew that it doesn't matter if it's your prospective boss or your children, when you know who you're communicating with, your can craft a message that will connect every time.

PANEL RESULTS

Diana phoned me after meeting with the interview panel and confirmed she had hit this one out of the park. As she was presenting, she was careful to press the buttons of each panel member and speak to their personal preferences. Their heads nodded throughout the interview, and she could see she was reaching each person while still conveying all of the information about her skills and experience. Diana walked out of that room feeling confident she was a front runner for the poison.

A few days later her instincts proved correct: she was offered the job and has since been promoted two more times in the past three years! Each time she is confronted with having to deliver a message to someone, she draws upon my coaching and is able to adjust the way she communicates that message to suit the style of person receiving it. This valuable skill has helped her rapidly advance her career to dizzying heights!

MBA (Mom's Business Acumen) Class: The Four Main Communication Styles

Understanding what makes people tick is a useful tool for getting positive results at work and at home. You can learn a lot about someone by watching them communicate and process ideas. This knowledge can arm you with vital information to improve your ability to negotiate, persuade, motivate and lead teams. Here are the main four communication styles I have observed:

1. **The Creative Thinker** — If you fall into this category you have an abundance of ideas. Your brain races and you can't turn the idea-machine off! You confidently share all

your ideas without editing or analyzing the viability of execution. You tend to overwhelm people sometimes with your confidence. You are direct and to-the-point, (some might call it "blunt"). Your ego is not too closely attached to your ideas because you have so many. "Don't like this one? Wait until you hear my next idea!" The best way to handle this communication style is to get to the point: if you beat around the bush, you'll lose them.

2. **The Doubting Thomas** — This person will poke a hole in every plan, though usually their intent is pure. They want to be sure there are no mistakes made, and they are very thorough and process-oriented. They will push you to examine every possible outcome. They have tendencies toward perfectionism: a project will never be ready to launch in their eyes. They also have difficulty making a decision and need lots of time for a complete analysis of the situation. They are great to have on a team because they will think of situations that could go wrong and give you time to make some preventative plans. Just don't let them slow the process down for too long.

3. **The Salesman** — Salesmen are the polar opposite to the Doubting Thomas. The salesman is all about quick, uncomplicated bursts of information. They are more focused on the relationship than the data. They are not very detail-oriented and need a good assistant to get work done, and they always know where to get resources. They are a connector and are critical for advancing a project once the plan has been made. They tend to frustrate others due to the fact that they do not seem to be paying attention to the conversation or

instructions, but they are mostly just focusing on how they can contribute in an overview of the project by selling the idea to others for contributions, funding, sponsorship or resources.

4. **The Soldier** — Every organization needs a soldier (or ten). These are the people who actually execute the work. They are list makers and very detail-oriented. They usually will not buck authority but will just bear down and get the job done. They are quiet and introverted. You will only need to tell them an instruction one time (if you tell them again it's an insult!) and the work gets done. They have difficulty coming up with an innovative solution, but will happily make sure your idea gets completed to perfection.

Now take some time to examine your team in respect to these four categories, and use the descriptions above to alter your message and communicate with them more clearly. By using this information as a guide, you'll be getting the best out of your team in no time!

CHAPTER 10

STAND UP

PICTURE OF ME

Learning how to stand up for yourself and be your own advocate — while still being modest — is a delicate skill to learn. Understanding that we are all responsible for taking charge of our own lives is a pivotal piece of our personal development.

Growing up, I was a pleasant and happy child, but I was also timid. As the oldest in my family, I had no experience dealing with kids who were older than I. When I was in middle school, I was intimidated by the children in the grades above me, so I usually tried to just blend into the background, hoping no one would notice me.

Although I still see myself as that soft, gentle girl, I am also a professional woman with twenty-five years of experience in the business world. I've learned to project less of that vulnerable person and more of the powerful person I've become. That confidence comes through in how I communicate and how I come across to others. Honesty is the core of my professional self, and being honest with colleagues and clients often translates into a perception that I am intense and that I push hard when I feel very strongly about something. I am tuned into people's feelings and intuitively, I sense when people are feeling confused, joyful, or in turmoil.

My mother was an incredible role model for the virtues of being a good person and being considerate of others. She taught me the importance of focusing on who you are rather than what you do or accomplish. She gave me tools to make peace with the adversity in my life through faith and strength. My father always believed I could do anything I set my mind to...even when I didn't believe it myself. And I married a man who had that same strong belief in my ability to accomplish anything.

"CAN'T" ISN'T A WORD

When my children were four and five-years-old, my husband Rich and I took them to the local high school running track to ride their bicycles. When we arrived, to our dismay the gate around the track was locked. Rich wasn't deterred, and he easily lifted the kids over the fence as he asked me to do the same with their bicycles. I thought the bikes were too heavy for me to lift, so I replied, "I can't." I've never seen Rich get so angry with me before!

"Don't tell me you can't. They're not that heavy, and you're strong. You can get them over the fence," he told me. I repeated I couldn't do it, and he refused to accept my excuses. We got into such a fight, arguing back and forth over what I could and could not do. Suddenly, I was standing back on that rooftop with Captain Evil yelling at me to jump off the building. And just as in that moment, I again heard the voices of my mother, aunts and grandmother telling me that I could do anything I wanted to, whether it was as terrifying as jumping off a building or as simple as lifting a few bicycles over a fence. Empowered by their voices, I hauled the bikes over the fence one by one. I stood there astonished as he smiled at me. "I told you that you could do it. You're the strongest person I know." Our anger melted away, and I felt a sense of accomplishment wash over me. Maybe Rich, my father, and the wonderful women in my life were right: I really *could* do anything. This moment was another true turning point for me.

Between my father believing I could accomplish anything, my mother believing that just by existing I had value, and my life partner constantly challenging me to be everything I could be…I had no choice but to grow into the strength and power that had always existed inside of me. Standing in my own power was more than just accepting I could do things if I wanted to; it was being able to push myself out of my comfortable places.

Lipstick Leadership

"Both of my grandmothers taught in one-room school-houses in rural Pennsylvania for many years. I visited those schoolhouses with them in the '50s and '60s and was amazed at how self-sufficient they were. My mother started her own kindergarten — also in Pennsylvania in the '50s — and then taught in an elementary school for another 35 years. The lessons that I learned from them are those of perseverance and determination to finish the job in spite of all obstacles and hardships which you many encounter both at home and in the workplace."

~ Kati Machtley, Women's Summit Director,
  Bryant University

**Submit your best "Mom's Wisdom" story at
www.LipstickLeadership.com today!**

We all navigate through the ups and downs of life. Whether or not you let them beat you depends on how you see them and what you choose to do about them. Do you choose to use adversity as fuel...or as an excuse? In the face of an obstacle, do you shut down or stand up and fight? You choose. We all have to take responsibility for our actions. It's easy to play the blame game and take the quitter's way out, but the life that results isn't much of a life at all.

So how does a timid little girl become a confident woman? By standing up and facing her fears! Most people think only powerful people can acquire great wealth, success and influence. I disagree. I believe we all have the power to get anything we want if we are brave enough to choose to get past our fear. Fear is what holds us back from everything we desire.

TRAGEDY IN NEW YORK

Twenty-five years ago, I knew a young woman who had just graduated from college and was working in New York City. She commuted to work everyday from her basement apartment about forty-five minutes north of the city. Every day she took the train through Westchester and the Bronx into Grand Central Station where she switched to the cross-town subway that brought her to Times Square where she *then* hopped on a local subway to bring her downtown to the financial district and her office. It was quite a commute!

This young woman worked for a large computer company as a corporate sales representative. Out of a sales force of fifty, she was the first — and the only — woman sales rep they'd ever hired. Her sales territory included the Towers of the World Trade Center and about twenty blocks in each direction. The competition was fierce, both with other companies and within her office, but this young woman held her own and excelled at her job.

One morning when she was on her way to work, she had a life-altering experience. As she was coming up the steps of the subway, busily running through the day's to do list, she was struck in the temple by a briefcase with such force that she blacked out.

When she regained consciousness in an alley three blocks away from the subway, she was alone, wearing torn clothes, her face smashed and swollen and her ribs broken. In shock, she moved on autopilot out of the alley and back to the subway. She retraced the route back to her apartment, barely aware of the curious and concerned stares of the other subway riders. When she arrived home, she locked the door behind her and caught her reflection in a mirror as she passed by. Seeing the dried blood and bruises on her face, she began to realize what had happened to her. She tried to piece together the events as she showered, trying to wash off what her attacker had done to her.

The young woman ascertained that in the flow of the crowd coming up the subway stairs, her attacker hit her without being noticed and then pretended to be a "good Samaritan" assisting an obviously sick woman up and out of the subway entrance. He must have dragged her those three blocks to the alley where he then beat and raped her, leaving her there when he was through.

Instead of seeking medical attention, the young woman went to her church and sat for hours praying for the strength to overcome this tragedy and giving thanks for her life that was remarkably spared. When she returned to her apartment, a co-worker was waiting there, concerned when she didn't show up for work. She told him that she had been mugged on the subway, and he immediately offered to help her in any way he could. She asked him to drive her to her beloved aunt's house, knowing it was a safe haven and knowing that her aunt would provide her with the strength and comfort she needed to get through this horrifying event.

After three days with her aunt, healing, praying and drawing upon her aunt's strength, the young woman made a series of choices that set a course for her life. She chose to return to work, riding the subway as she always had. She chose to be a survivor rather than a victim, refusing to be afraid of leaving her home. She chose to live her life rather than letting this horrible event turn her into a frightened shell of a person. How did she find the courage to go back into the city so soon after her attack? She knew somewhere inside of her existed an incredible strength of will to overcome any fear that threatened to overtake her. She had conquered a great fear in the past — a debilitating fear of heights — and she knew she could do it again.

I know this story is true because I was that young woman.

OVERCOMING FEAR

Fear is one of the most limiting factors in most people's lives. It prevents you from achieving your highest potential in any aspect of your life. Overcoming any situation you are afraid of increases your power until FEAR as a mindset is gone. Once you have pushed past through any fear—big or small—you know that you can "do" fear. You conquer it, instead of letting it control you. It is not so much getting past fear as such, but removing it from your being. Then, your mind is open to the possibilities for success that are truly endless.

Confronting your fears — big and small — will be the best gift you can give yourself. However, it is easier if you confront and conquer your small fears first. Armed with these triumphs, you'll be able to handle any monstrous, unimaginable fears that could lie ahead. Learn who you are and what you are made of before you find yourself immersed in a state of severe trauma. This prepares you to push your way through anything: the loss of a loved one, physical danger, health issues, or even career and relationship pressures. You'll never let fear or tragedy win when you know you can get through anything life throws at you.

Each time you overcome a fear, you empower yourself to be able to overcome another fear. It's a cumulative effect. Had I never overcome my fear of heights at twenty as I rappelled off the science building, I might not have thought I was strong enough to survive the fear of walking around New York City at twenty-three. I might not have been able to tap into that confidence or believe I could do it. Strength and faith prepares you for future challenges great and small.

When I think about doing something I'm afraid of, I look back on rappelling off that building because it's very positive example of my strength. I know I own my power and my strength, but I also know I am not alone in this, and I often turn to prayer as well. I pray for the strength to be able to continue to see the world as a positive place.

It's important not to wait for the big catastrophes in life to test your mettle. Prepare yourself by overcoming fears everyday and continually growing your strength. Take control over your fears in any way you know how. For me, it's through prayer. Mimi gave me that gift through the example of her faith. She has a light in her that she credits to her spirituality, and I am blessed to have that gift as well to help me stand up when I need to. No matter which

way works best for you, the most important point is that you find
your own life and stand up for yourself!

Simple Truth from Mom:
Find your power by overcoming your fear!

In every tragic moment we have an opportunity to
learn more about who we are and what we are capa-
ble of in our lives. When you're at a point that is
vulnerable, you're also at your most authentic. If
there is a positive that can come from tragedy, it's the
opportunity to meet yourself and recognize the power
you have within. The knowledge that I can overcome
fear has served me well throughout my life, even
when I'm shaking in my boots! What a blessing that
awareness has been for me.

MY PROFESSIONAL PERSONA

Personally and professionally, I am the culmination of all my
life experiences. Every event, every tragedy, every triumph in my
life has given me strength to take on any challenge. You might be
surprised to know that I would not change anything about my
life...I like the woman I have become, and to change anything is
to change the essence of Michelle. I am a successful business-
woman because I have learned to push past any fear, overcome
any obstacle. The nurturing voices of the women in my life
constantly remind me that I have everything I need for success,
no matter what might stand in the way.

However, no matter where my professional life takes me, my art is my rock and my well. From it, I draw my strength, and as I have grown as an artist, my art has become an incredible tool for my work, the metaphor of me professionally. When I start to feel overwhelmed I turn to my art. It brings me to a completely fear-less place and amplifies the words of the women in my life. When I paint, fear, reluctance and inhibition are stripped away—I am completely in control and powerful, and I love to feel that way!

FINDING POWER IN MY ART

Within my art and the artistic process, I find the power that is Michelle. The act of painting is therapeutic and allows me the time to focus not on my business, my writing, a speech, my family, or my household, but on my emotional state of being and my creative self. I delve into that quiet time and listen to the voices of the women in my past, encouraging me and guiding me, I am able to press forward through any problem or obstacle or fear.

The *way* I paint in and of itself is a source of power. It can best be described as "controlled chaos." This phrase also characterizes how I coach, manage my business, clean, cook, love and live my life. If you come into my studio with me to paint — and I do this sometimes with business clients who are feeling stuck creatively when facing an issue in their career or business — this is what you will find:

First, you'll be overwhelmed by the vivid colors of about twenty half-finished paintings hanging on the white walls! Also in the room are a couple of wooden easels with blank canvases ready to go, a trundle bed with a paint-splattered comforter, jugs brimming with brushes and palette knives, containers of sand and rocks, and a laundry basket overflowing with paints. There seems to be chaos in this room, but all I see is peace and tranquility and my space to create! I get lost in time when I walk through the door, and as I paint, the room becomes a blur of art and artist.

As we get started with the artistic journey, I will ask you to look into my paint basket and see what colors are speaking to you. I look for whatever color is calling me that day and bring the tube of paint to the canvas it is meant for; sometimes it's a blank canvas and sometimes it's one of the unfinished works on my wall. I immediately start applying the paints directly to the canvas, mixing them right there with my hands. Because I know the "system" and technique of my art, I can jump right into the execution phase without sacrificing quality. If the spirit moves me, I add other elements of nature — like the sand and rocks and even the leaves from my plants — to my paintings to create textures and shapes. I paint until I feel the session is done for the day. Tomorrow, I'll come back and do the same thing.

My work is abstract, created by the fluid movements of my hands. Many of my paintings give the illusion of water, not surprising considering I grew up on the water and live by the water. But this water isn't what I'm seeing out the window; it's the emotions swirling around deep inside of me. Ironically, while this kind of chaos fuels my style of painting, many times the end product projects tranquility. The tone of the painting transforms depending upon where I am emotionally at that moment in time. As I work the paint into the canvas, I work through the joy and fears in my life, moving toward my power with every stroke.

Painting is a process of discovery and letting everything inside me emerge. I painted after I got the call my beloved Aunt Marie had passed away. The size of the canvas was huge because the feeling I had was huge. The colors changed as my grief transformed from pain into a celebration of the life of my Aunt Marie. The painting reflected my emotions and Aunt Marie's powerful influence.

Recently, I was commissioned to do eight paintings at a parish center in Connecticut. This work was a prayerful expression of my emotions. It was especially meaningful work for me because it is hanging in a place of worship and community service. Exhibiting my paintings takes a degree of fearlessness because my paintings are a snapshot of who I am on the inside: sometimes raw but always real. But as you know, I know how to *jump* so I pushed past the fear of my artwork being criticized and I presented those paintings to the parish. The positive response was overwhelming, and I was so thankful that I hadn't let fear rob me of it.

Lipstick Leadership

"My grandmother, Sally Hegle, was married in the 1930s. My grandparents had a farm during the depression and the dustbowl years in the Midwest (North Dakota). When I was young, I thought my grandmother 'just stayed at home.' But she was an entrepreneur — it wasn't obvious to me. She taught me to work hard so you can play hard; to use what you have (including your brain); to save part of what you have, no matter how hard it might seem at the time; and to never give up.

"When my grandparents couldn't make a go of the farm because of a serious drought, my grandfather traveled wherever he could to find work, leaving my grandmother behind with a baby, a cow and a dried up farm. My grandmother tied the baby to her chest, put a rope around the cow's neck and walked up and down the ditches on the sides of the road because that was the only green grass around. My grandmother used to chuckle when she told the story because she said it must have been quite a sight.

"My grandparents made it through the Depression and were able to keep the farm. After that experience, my grandmother raised chickens, had a huge garden and apple orchard and used to take her eggs and produce into town to sell when my grandfather took the milk to the creamery to sell. She said she never wanted to go hungry again, and she didn't.

"My grandmother is ninety-five today and last year successfully underwent knee replacement surgery because she didn't want to live the rest of her life in a wheel chair. I was luck to have spent many summers with Grandma Sally, who taught me about work, integrity and love."

~ Julie Viskup, Law Professor at Champlain College

THE ARTIST'S COACHING PROCESS

In my art, I have a tendency to be a little messy. At a glance, my coaching might appear to have that same quality; however, my art has a consistent process that brings out the insight and instinct in me as an artist, and my coaching also has a consistent process that brings out the insight and instinct in me as a strategist. And just as I use my art to find my inner power and overcome my fears, I employ a unique coaching technique designed to do the same for my clients.

When I work with a client, I don't use the standardized tests that many other coaches use. I find at the executive level, most clients have already completed these tests but have not figured out how to use the data to affect change in their work environment. The first step in my coaching process is observation. I will shadow a client, observing them in their natural habitat, before I interview them and their subordinates, peers, up-line management and sometimes even their customers.

This particular system is different than a traditional 360 survey; in a 360 survey, a questionnaire is floated to your boss, your co-workers and your subordinates. They're asked to provide feedback on how you do your job and what it's like to work with and for you. I find I can gather more information in a conversation than through a survey, and I'm able to draw out more of the subtle nuances in the client's relationships and how they perform the "communication dance." Without this valuable perspective, my clients may find themselves blocked from achieving their desired outcomes at work. After I go through this whole process, we create a "threads" report that shows them the trends and common themes from the information I've gathered, rather than the actual responses from each person. This keeps the possibility of one person's opinion or statement derailing a client to a minimum.

Lipstick Leadership

"I remember when my mother was fifty, she took a class at the local university with a bunch of students in their early twenties. It was a class on ecology, and towards the end, there was field work that involved a day-long hike up a mountain. I remember my mother being nervous about it; I also remember the energy that radiated from her when she got home late that night, having completed the trip successfully.

"She said that the other students had encouraged her. I don't honestly know whether she fell behind, or by how far, or what it took to get her through that day. But what I do know is that there was a lesson in there about pushing yourself to do things that you want to do and also about being satisfied with your personal best. It is okay to be afraid or nervous about doing something you want to do — as long as you don't let that fear stop you. I draw on that in my own life. And of course, now

that I'm close to fifty, I have a better sense of what she was going through. (But isn't 50 the new 30?!)."

~ Regina Maruca, Former Harvard Business Review Editor and Co-Author of "The Leadership Legacy"

Submit your best "Mom's Wisdom" story at www.LipstickLeadership.com today!

The way I work with clients can be characterized as more of a strategy session than a coaching session. I draw from the client their goals and outcomes. Then we start to do a little bit of an organizational anthropology. We dig into the structure of organization, its values, who the players are, and the underlying dynamics that can't be captured in a traditional organization chart. We discover who *really* has the influence and who can help the client advance. We do the same type of study with the type of work they're doing. We discuss the outcome of their projects in regards to impacting the organization and what exposure opportunities they might be missing. Next, we analyze team dynamics and the skill sets of both themselves and their team.

As we take a look at all of these elements, we start to create a picture of what the client's reality looks like. Solutions start to emerge and become clear to both myself and to the client, and we look at the strategies that can help them be successful. It isn't just about looking at today; it's about looking at yesterday and tomorrow, too, to get the clearest picture of the client's situation. Then, we work together to choose a path for the client.

My coaching method is proactive and results-driven. It's customized and focuses on the day-to-day reality and the interpretation of data gathered. Success comes when the client sees the amazing possibilities for advancement in their career or business if they think strategically and creatively and act tactically and organized. It takes confidence and a comfort level with risk for a client to take action, and I'm continually proud of the work my team and I do to help my clients overcome their fears and advance their careers. I guess the clients are happy, too, judging by the amazing success we've have over the last fifteen years!

NEW FEARS TO OVERCOME

Coaching isn't the only aspect of my business that consumes my time and tests my ability to push past fears. As a professional speaker, I press the limits of my comfort zone every time I step out onto a stage in front of a sea of people. Even after twenty-plus years, I still feel the butterflies flitting around in my stomach before a presentation! However, I've learned to channel that nervous energy about conveying my message. The stage becomes a place that I feel the same expressive freedom that I do when I paint. Fear does not exist in that place!

Becoming an author also brought forth a new realm of fears. What if I didn't have the talent to write? What if I couldn't express all of the amazing wisdom I've gathered from the women in my life over the years? What if I'm simply not cut out to be an author? I tossed and turned many a night pondering those questions before I finally pushed through those fear barriers and threw myself into my writing. Sitting down in front of a blank screen watching that cursor blink was as terrifying as presenting to an auditorium full of CEOs, but I drew upon the strength and power of my creativity and started tapping away at the keyboard anyway. After a few lines of typing "All work and no play makes Michelle a dull girl," to set me at ease, I began the process of funneling my creativity through the written word and *From the Kitchen* was born.

One of the fears that both my speaking and authoring have brought to the surface is my fear for safety when traveling alone. My work in both capacities takes me all over the country and abroad to Europe and Asia, addressing corporations, speaking at conferences and working with entrepreneurs. All that traveling to strange cities pushes my comfort level, but as you well know, I like a good challenge! Each time I go into a new city, I'm confronted with old fears, but I don't let them stop me from traveling alone, staying at hotels and using public transportation. If I wasn't aware of my own power and my ability to push past my fears, I would be missing out on so many experiences and opportunities. My career path would be completely different, and I doubt I would be able to earn my living performing the work that I find tremendously rewarding and joyful.

I challenge my clients to work through their pain and fears to find their power, just as I have done. It's not easy, and sometimes it's not pretty, but it's *always* worth the work. Now I'd like to challenge YOU! What are you afraid of, and what amazing things is it keeping you from achieving?

MBA (Mom's Business Acumen) Class: Managing Your Fear Checklist

If you want to develop the ability to manage your fear, here is what worked for me and the hundreds of clients I've worked with:

Step 1: **Identify something that is not life-threatening that you are afraid of.** One of my fears as a teenager was speaking in front of groups (ironic, I am a professional speaker now). I also was very afraid of heights as a young adult (truth be told, I'm still not so hot on high places).

Step 2: **Answer what confronting the fear makes you feel.** My fear of heights would make me feel dizzy, short of breath and sometimes actually sick to my stomach. I would then start to feel weak and vulnerable — and very afraid. That feeling of fear sometimes would control my actions and how engaged I was in an activity. It made me feel powerless. If I let the fear control me, I'd miss out on a lot of great stuff in my life like hikes up mountains, restaurants with a window view, and athletic activities with friends and family.

Step 3: **Visualize yourself pushing past your fear taking control of the situation.** Before I rappelled down the side of that building in college, I often tried to visualize myself succeeding at being in high places, and the mere thought of being more than a foot off the ground made me dizzy and nauseous! I would bail out of my pretend confrontation; it was too scary and uncomfortable. Then I began to get angry at myself for being so afraid.

"It's all in your mind," I thought. "Just push past it!" I continued to practice my visualizations, picturing myself at the top of a mountain looking down and fighting the fear that threatened to overwhelm me. This exercise was another step in overcoming my fear and was part of my success later on.

Step 4: **Find an opportunity to confront your fear.** You heard me right: seek out something you're afraid of and push yourself through it! Although my ROTC final exam found me rather than me finding it, it was still an opportunity that presented itself and one that I (eventually) took advantage of. At the time, I was in a panic. I felt all of the physical pain that literally being on the edge would bring to someone afraid of heights: dizziness, sweating, feeling sick to my stomach, my heart pounding in my chest...but when I finally went over the side and stood at the bottom looking up, it was worth all the pain. I knew I would be able to do anything I set my mind to because I jumped off a building!

Step 5: **Just do it!** I jumped off a building — now it's your turn!

By following these steps and overcoming my fear of heights, I found the strength to push through much tougher problems in my life. This event taught me that I was more powerful than I gave myself credit for and filled me with the steely resolve to overcome any fear or adversity in the future. It's not that I've never been afraid again; it's just that I know I can get past those fears. No fear will ever control me, and knowing that has helped me persevere through any obstacle that gets in my way.

Lipstick Leadership

"It is very fun for me to balance what my mother has taught me with what you, Michelle, have taught me. In addition to the many business lessons you have taught me, the lesson that stands out the most in my mind is the lesson of bringing play into the workplace. When I painted with you and watched you bake bread, I saw this whole other side of you. This side did not reconcile at first with the passionate, bold business woman and mentor you had become for me. As we dove deeper into the creative process, it became clear that your painting was like my filmmaking...a calling. As I watched you paint and reflect on my business needs, I saw how your used your art playfully to work through abstract problems and fuel your imagination keeping you mentally sharp. Your lesson of play helps inspire me when I get to a place where creatively I need fuel."

~ Shalini Kantayya, Activist/Film Director,
   www.ADropofLife.com

**Advance your career with the help of
Michelle's FREE e-zine. Sign up today at
www.LipstickLeadership.com!**

The next time you're feeling overcome by fear, remember these steps and push through it to the overwhelming sense of accomplishment on the other side!

CHAPTER 11

BECOMING THE FAMILY BREAD MAKER

BREAD BAKING HISTORY

As I stand in my kitchen and cook, I am surrounded by the nurturing voices of generations of amazing women. The aroma of freshly baked bread instantly transports me back to my Aunt Jennie's tiny kitchen. Suddenly, I'm standing at her kitchen table once again, staring down at a mess of flour, yeast, and water in my hands, wondering how it will ever become a loaf of bread.

As an immigrant from Torre Di Ruggiero in Italy, Giovanna Yozzo Fanelli came to this country with her parents in 1919. Her family had very little but carved out a life for themselves in the outskirts of New York City. Jennie was the only daughter and with that came the responsibility of helping her mother with the cooking and cleaning for her father and three brothers. Though she couldn't have children of her own, Jennie was a mother figure to her brother Frank's children (my father and Aunt Marie) and to their children and to their children's children. We all have fond memories of Jennie, a four foot drill sergeant with her "white glove inspections." Her joking sarcasm was almost as legendary as her skill in the kitchen. Until her death a few years ago (at the age of 97!), Jennie was our family's keeper of recipes and traditions.

Lipstick Leadership

"My mom taught me to try new things and improvise. Mom's acts of daring tended to happen in the kitchen — she'd find a recipe for bouillabaisse that took five hours and she'd find a way to make it in forty minutes. Or she'd take a fat-laden recipe for chicken and change a few ingredients to make a tasty, simpler and healthier version. She was never afraid to experiment. I'm not as daring as my mother in the kitchen, but I think her confidence shows up in my work as a book coach. I'm comfortable trying new things and applying them to my

work for clients. I credit my mom with that ability to take something new and tweak it for my own purposes."

~ Lisa Tener, Book Coach

Submit your best "Mom's Wisdom" story at www.LipstickLeadership.com today!

One of the traditions Aunt Jennie brought with her to this new world was her talent for cooking and baking, particularly her delicious homemade bread: golden and crusty on the outside, soft and chewy on the inside. Generations of our family have clamored for this bread and not a holiday passed when it wasn't present on our table. I spent years breaking her bread and dipping it in olive oil or — if she wasn't looking — in the pasta sauce. When I ventured out into the world on my own, I knew I wanted to be able to carry on her delectable tradition in my own home.

THE FIRST LESSON

After I graduated college, I landed my job as the first female sales representative for a computer company in Manhattan. Because living in the city was unbelievably expensive even then, I found a cozy apartment in the same town as my Nana and my beloved Aunt Jennie. Being on my own meant leaving the delicious cooking of my mother behind, and rather than starve or try to subsist on Ramen noodles, I decided to take advantage of the master cooking instructor I had in my own backyard: Aunt Jennie.

Aunt Jennie agreed to be my cooking guru, and one spring morning, I showed up at the two-family house where she lived upstairs, ready to learn how to bake her marvelous bread. I walked up to the landing and heard a familiar voice call out from above. Because she wasn't as nimble as she used to be, Aunt Jennie would wait at the window for company, and when they arrived, she would open the window and toss down a crumpled brown bag that held a rock (to weight it down) and her house keys. The visitor would have to be ready to catch Aunt Jennie's bag or risk getting beaned in the head with it!

That morning I was lucky enough to catch the bag and not a concussion, and I used the keys to let myself in. As I climbed the stairs to her apartment, I breathed in its familiar scent, a blend of Aunt Jennie's pasta sauce, her anisette cookies, and her Jean Nate perfume! Aunt Jennie was waiting at the top of the stairs in the doorway with an excited and mischievous gleam in her eyes. We hugged and kissed and then she shooed me into the kitchen to get started right away.

Laid out on her tiny table were all of her silver canisters, bowls, and a few utensils. I recognized them from the hundreds of times I was part of the kitchen brigade responsible for holiday feasts. In fact, I felt pretty confident in myself that baking bread would be no problem; after all, I'd helped out so many times before, how hard could it be?

As I tied an apron around my waist, I looked over the goods on the table, searching for the scrap of paper that would contain the secret recipe for Aunt Jennie's bread. It wasn't there. *Maybe Aunt Jennie wants to hand it over to me with a little ceremony or something*, I thought with a smile. Jennie joined me at the table and started opening her canisters for me, and not only did I not see any recipe, I noticed Aunt Jennie wasn't even using measuring cups or spoons!

"Aunt Jennie, where's the recipe?" I asked. She only laughed and shook her head, obviously amused I would think there was a written recipe for her magical bread...or that she would make it so easy for me to learn how to make it.

See, my little powerhouse aunt believed in the importance of hard work. She was an immigrant who came to this country with very little. She relied on her determination, her will, and her talents to carve out a life for herself. Rather than become bitter about her struggles and losses, she had faith in whatever the future would hold. To her, working hard for something meant truly appreciating it, becoming skilled at it, and enjoying the satisfaction and confidence that came with mastering it. So if I wanted her secret recipe, I was going to have to EARN IT!

Under her eagle eye, I heaped handfuls of flour and pinches of salt into a huge ceramic bowl, creating a mountain of powdery snow, always looking for a nod of approval from her. In another bowl, I mixed warm water — no thermometer, of course — and yeast. Aunt Jennie instructed me on how to tell if the yeast was good and ran my hand under the water so I could gauge its temperature. She watched as I made a well in the center of the flour and poured the yeast mixture in it. Then the really hard work began. Aunt Jennie pantomimed how to draw the flour into the center and start incorporating the ingredients together, "Use your hands, touch and hold. You will know when is nice-nice," then she stepped away and watched me try. I called to mind all of the times I'd watched her bake as a child: she'd provided me with a model for success in the kitchen; now I just needed to follow it.

After a few moments, I was up to my elbows in a sticky paste that looked nothing like the smooth ball of dough for her bread. Exasperated, I pulled my hands out of the bowl and asked, "Aunt Jennie, how in the world is *that* ever going to become bread?" She sighed and shook her head at me before pushing me aside and dipping her hands into the mixture. Within minutes, the dough was in a beautiful smooth ball!

I stood there dumfounded and she gave me a little pinch. "You need to be stronger, Michelina! My mother, she use thirty pounds of flour! This nothing! You need to put muscle into it!" And so we repeated the process with another ten pounds of flour to make more bread. Every time, I would get tired of kneading before the dough came together and Aunt Jennie would have to take over; a few quick kneads later and the dough was perfect once again. After the dough rose FOUR TIMES, we put it in the oven, and soon we were enjoying her magnificent bread.

I left Aunt Jennie's house feeling confident that after a few trips to the gym to build up my arm muscles, I'd be able to master her recipe on my own! The ingredients seemed simple enough, and so were the techniques she'd taught me. I could already picture slicing into my own loaf of bread…and maybe even sharing it with a cute boy.

SOLO MISSION

The weekend following my bread baking lesson with Aunt Jennie, I decided I was going to impress her by making a loaf of her bread all by myself. I breezed into the grocery store, headed up the baking aisle…and stopped in my tracks in front of the flour. There before me were at least a dozen different kinds of flour! Wheat flour, rye flour, all purpose flour, cake flour, self-rising flour…and here I thought flour was just flour! I stood there for twenty minutes pick up and putting down bags until I finally decided "all purpose" was the way to go. I picked up the yeast next and was thankful to find there was really only one kind to choose!

Back at my apartment, I regained the confidence I lost at the supermarket and got down to work. Without any measurements to go by, I did my best to remember the height of the flour mountain, the number of salt pinches, the amount and warmth of the water, and how many drizzles of oil Aunt Jennie's recipe called for. I kneaded and kneaded and kneaded until the dough miraculously came together just like Aunt Jennie's! I was so proud as I set it aside to rise that I thought about calling Aunt Jennie and telling her I'd be at her door with a fresh loaf of bread this afternoon, but I decided it would be better to surprise her.

An hour and half passed and I happily checked on the dough to find…it hadn't risen at all! I was devastated and phoned her in tears. "Aunt Jennie, I don't know what happened! I did everything you said and I think I used the right amount of everything, and it didn't rise!" Between my own crying and her broken English, I couldn't understand a word she was saying, so I drove over to her house.

We sat down at her table together with tea and pieces of her heavenly biscotti, and I explained everything I did in detail. She nodded along and said finally, "Should be nice-nice." Then she thought for a moment and asked, "What kind yeast you use?"

"The dry yeast that comes in red and yellow packets of three," I replied.

Aunt Jennie shook her head and smiled, "Is no good. Go to your bakery and talk to the baker. He give you a nice slice of fresh yeast. You cut into pieces like this," she motioned with her hands. "And freeze the rest. Use fresh yeast, next time, bread be better." I thanked her and hugged her good-bye before heading home to toss out my useless lump of dough.

The next weekend I drove to three different bakeries before tracking down a baker who would sell me some of his fresh yeast. I cut it into cubes just like Aunt Jennie told me to and went about the dough-making process once again. This time I knew it would work out, and lo and behold, when I checked to see if the dough had risen, it had! Excitedly, I punched it down and kneaded it for a moment longer before plopping it into the oven.

When the timer dinged, I giddily pulled out the loaf...and noticed it seemed to weigh a ton! *Maybe it's just the pan I'm using,* I thought uncertainly. But no: after the bread cooled, I cut a slice and knew immediately this bread was nothing like Jennie's. It was hard, dense and missing the subtle flavor I knew it should have.

I didn't burst into tears; this time I was a little angry with Aunt Jennie. She obviously had "forgotten" to tell me something about her recipe and I didn't appreciate it one bit. I marched over to her house and complained to her. She yelled at me, "Is no my fault you no follow directions! Tell me what you did." So again I explained the steps — "Just like you showed me, Aunt Jennie" — and again she nodded along.

"What did flour look like?" she asked. Confused, I said, "Well…it was white…and powdery…it was all-purpose…."

She shook her head at me, "No good. No good. Go to pork store [an Italian deli and grocery near her building] and buy special flour. Makes it rise nice-nice with yeast." After a few more questions, I ascertained she meant I should buy bread flour and after another cup of tea, biscotti and a hug, I returned to my apartment to once again toss out my bread failure.

JUST LIKE AUNT JENNIE'S!

It took a few more tries and a few more trips to Aunt Jennie's for clarification before I finally got her bread recipe right. When I felt like giving up, like I didn't have the same talent for bread baking, like the mess in front of me would never become a crusty masterpiece, I heard Aunt Jennie's voice coaxing me to succeed. "Don't give up, Michelina. Never give up when you so close. Keep working; you have what you need to make good bread." In my mind and during a few times when I attempted to bake bread with her at her home again, she hovered beside me, watching patiently and gently steering (and sometimes pinching and poking) me in the right direction, but never giving away too much and *never* doing it for me. I knew I had to be brave enough to try on my own and to go back to my guru with questions. I studied how the ingredients (and how much I used of them) impacted the quality of my bread. I discovered the subtle improvements a master baker like Aunt Jennie would know. I became the bread and the baker.

Finally, one afternoon I pulled a steaming loaf from the oven and sliced into it. It was just as good as Aunt Jennie's! I was so excited I raced over to her apartment with a piece to present to her for inspection. She took a bite while I held my breath. "Il pane è perfetto," she said with a proud smile, and I was flooded with the feelings of accomplishment and confidence in my own abilities. With Aunt Jennie as my mentor, her belief in me, and her guidance, I was able to use the tools and resources I had within myself to succeed at being a bread baker. As I became confident in my own abilities and my understanding of technique and ingredients, I started adding my own twists to the basic Italian bread Aunt Jennie groomed me to bake, adding roasted peppers, sun-dried tomatoes, rosemary, and caramelized onions. Because of her, I was brave enough to try new things and take the bread into different directions. I created bread that was distinctly my own to pass down to my nieces, sons, and grandchildren. I grew into a baker that Aunt Jennie would be proud of.

For Aunt Jennie, it was never really about the bread itself; it was about teaching me to succeed on my own. She was a master craftsman and my role model. She presented a process to build on and fostered my confidence to work with new ingredients. She guided me, and she taught me to rely on my instincts, my talents, and my self to succeed. Without her mentorship, I wouldn't have even known where to begin, and even though all of the elements of success where there, I needed Aunt Jennie to care enough to guide me and empower me.

Simple Truth from Mom:
Mentoring and preparing the next generation for
greatness is every leader's responsibility.

Aunt Jennie taught me that a leader provides her
people with the tools for success and teaches them
how to rely on themselves to reach a goal. A leader
encourages the team to work through failures and
setbacks fearlessly; to learn from each experience;
and to bring a deeper understanding of their individual talents and skills to the next challenge. A leader
also provides her team with a model, encourages
them to follow the model and, once learned, embrace
the possibility of personal creativity or deviation.
These lessons have served me well in growing my
corporate team and in advising my clients on how to
do the same with their teams.

Lipstick Leadership

"As young girls, my twin sister and I loved to watch our
mother dress for a function before she went out with
my father. We would behold her beautiful, tall frame
perfectly wrapped in any one of her saris from her vast
collection. My most sensual childhood memories

include my sister and I burying our faces in the safe folds of those perfect pleats, inhaling the scent of Chanel ∞5 permeating the shimmering fabric.

"I owe my fashion career to precious afternoons spent with my mother as she unpacked her trunk of saris. Each sari had a story. There were several stories attached to each sari: who bought it for her, who presented it to her, what was the occasion for which it was bought, where she was when she first wore it. The beautiful light turquoise sari with a saffron border her father presented to her the day she immigrated to America was stained by the vermillion her mother wore in a round circle between her eyes as she embraced my mother tightly while she said goodbye. Then there was the white cotton sari with a pale green print that her sisters often borrowed right after she ironed it and starched it. She always knew it had been worn because of the red dusty edges that matched the earth of the town where she grew up. My aunts would always return it to her cupboard, neatly folded with the hope that she wasn't clever enough to notice.

"I've always loved how her saris punctuate milestones both mundane and momentous in her lifetime. Add to this the story of the silk. Every time she pulled a sari from her trunk, she would tell us whether it was woven in West Bengal or in Tamil Nadu, in Maharashtra or in Karnataka. Each sari was linked to a particular tradition that had a story, a story that narrated the craftsmanship of our native country, India. The

Dhaka silk tradition was nearly eradicated when the British chopped off the thumbs of the Bengali weavers so they would not compete with the colonial silk trade. The Kanchipuram silk, the King of all silks, hails from a glorious temple town where silk was woven to swathe the gods and goddesses in the most royal of robes. I think my first education of India's geography was told through the artistry of these weavers.

"It has always been the story and experience of a person, a work of art, or a place that keeps me riveted and curious. As the child of immigrant parents, retelling the story of India and its artisans is the gossamer thread spinning endlessly through my work. The stories of my mother's saris bring me closer to her joys, pains and discoveries, and are the seeds that sprouted into my own personal and artistic 'discovering' of India, a lifelong process, granting me the fortune of a fulfilling fashion career."

~ Swati Argade, Fashion Designer,
   www.swatiargade.com

Advance your career with the help of Michelle's FREE e-zine. Sign up today at www.LipstickLeadership.com!

MENTORING...AUNT JENNIE STYLE

In an effort to practice what I teach and grow my own business, I decided to attend a women's leadership conference in Texas a few years ago. On the second night at the retreat center, our group was treated to a very special event: a young filmmaker named Shalini Kantayya was premiering her documentary, *A Drop of Life.*

The fictional story, written by Shalini and based on factual research, was set in India and focused on the possibility of a water shortage in the future and the impact of such a disaster. The film was breathtaking in its visual style and its powerful message. The images she captured and the story she told in those images impressed me. This was a woman who had a distinct point of view and a considerable amount of talent to express those views. As an activist, Shalini used her film as a platform for her message. I hoped to speak with Shalini again before the retreat ended, but for the next few days, our paths failed to cross as we attended the conference programs. On the final day, the group had lunch together before the closing ceremonies, and just as I was about to get up and leave, Shalini approached my table.

Dressed in full Indian garb, this beautiful petite young woman began speaking with the person seated next to me. I waited for a break in their conversation and took the opportunity to introduce myself to Shalini. "I loved your film," I told her. "How do you plan to bring it to the public?" At the mention of her work, I could see her eyes sparkle with passion as she explained she was still working on distribution and was currently looking for funding while trying to grow her production company 7th Empire Media. An announcement was made at that moment telling everyone to adjourn to another room for the closing ceremonies. Before we parted ways, I pressed one of my business cards into Shalini's hand and said, "Call me. I think we should talk."

The retreat ended and before I knew it, I was on my way home to Connecticut. A week later I opened my e-mail inbox to find a message from Shalini. She wrote she was hoping we could speak or meet within the next few weeks to discuss my thoughts on her funding issue. I invited her to Connecticut for an in-person meeting. She heartily accepted.

IMMEDIATE CONNECTION

Shalini took a train from New York City, and as she confessed to me later, during the three hour ride to my neck of the woods in Connecticut, she wondered what the two of us would talk about for the six hours until her departing train. In my office awaiting her arrival, I found myself thinking the same thing! She is a single, twenty-something, Indian-American activist filmmaker from New York, and I'm a forty-something, Italian-American mother of two, wife of twenty-one years, and CEO of a consulting firm in suburban Connecticut. Could we possibly have enough in common to weather six hours together??

It turned out our concerns were completely unwarranted. From the moment Shalini stepped off the train and greeted me as enthusiastically as an old friend, our connection was powerful. Those six hours flew by, and over the course of the day, we learned a lot about each other and saw the many ways we could help each other.

Shalini did not come from an affluent family; rather, she was raised by a single mother who fled India with her daughters at the end of an unsuccessful marriage. In an effort to better understand her Indian heritage, Shalini embarked on a visit to the homeland of her parents. It was during this trip she received her calling as a filmmaker. While in a Tibetan monastic community, she witnessed over 800 monks praying a deep-throated chant in unison. The sight so captivated her, she suddenly began seeing the scene as though it were a movie. Using the Camcorder she had with her, Shalini began filming and took the first step on her journey to becoming a filmmaker. When she returned to the States, she studied filmmaking at NYU and in 2001, she received the William D. Fulbright Fellowship to make a movie about political street theater in India.

As Shalini shared this story with me, I was entranced by her passion for filmmaking and for the powerful messages she wanted to convey in her films. However, after learning more about what this filmmaker was seeking in a funding package and the current status of 7th Empire Media, I became concerned that while her vision was sweeping, her lack of business skills had the potential to keep her from making a quantum leap in her career and to keep her powerful film from making the kind of global impact she had created it for. Though she had secured a significant amount of money through her own creative funding ideas, she had yet to secure the funding that would provide distribution of the film. Rather than shopping and sightseeing as I had planned, we spent the day exploring the strategies for applying her existing talents and utilizing my recipe for success to ensure the business side of her filmmaking and production company would grow and thrive and her film would be screened on a global scale.

By the end of our day together, I had committed to mentoring Shalini for an hour each week, and she committed to following my business advice and reporting back to me. Our mentoring relationship was much like my relationship with Aunt Jennie during her bread baking tutorial. Just as Aunt Jennie guided me — but never did it for me — and forced me to look within myself for the tools to bake the perfect loaf of bread, I did the same for Shalini in order to assist her in the growth of her business.

Lipstick Leadership

"Brigadier Pat Foote influenced me when I was a 2nd lieutenant and trying to manage everything. She said, 'The sign of a leader is how well their people do when they are not there. Train your people, always tell them the result you want but don't dictate the how...let them surprise you with their ingenuity. Never micromanage. Trust them to do the job, but always check, check, check.' She then 'killed' me in the war games and had my sergeants take over — they did great and I learned to power down."

~ E. Adrienne van Dooren, The House That Faux Built

Submit your best "Mom's Wisdom" story at
www.LipstickLeadership.com today!

MENTORING THE FILMMAKER

Shalini and I met during weekly telephone sessions and occasional face-to-face sessions to check her progress on the "recipe" for her success. I made sure she was on the right track, answering her questions and prodding her in the right direction. We began by focusing on the development of a business plan for her fledgling company 7th Empire Media as well as a marketing campaign for *A Drop of Life*. I guided in her obtaining a network of contacts that would help her promote and advance her film company, and together we explored other areas crucial to her success: Internet marketing, communication skills, publicity, budgeting and financial projections. Shalini knew more about these areas than she thought, and with her talent coupled with my insights, we made a powerful team!

One of the possibilities for marketing her film was a series of personal speaking engagements combined with a screening of the film. Although she was very comfortable behind the camera, she was a bit hesitant to get out in front of people. "You can do this," I told her. "The key to a great speech is be able to tell stories — and we KNOW you can do that already!"

We discovered one of the most valuable assets in marketing her film was the intrigue of how she got started and her life story. Although Shalini was hesitant to air her personal life to rooms full of strangers, she was also willing to push past her fears. The success we'd already found through our mentoring sessions fueled her to take the risk and get out there in front of the audience. We filmed her speaking so she could self-critique as well as take advantage of my insights and observations. Rather than creating her speeches for her, I guided her in crafting them herself so they would harness her skill for telling a story and truly embody everything she experienced in her life. She needed to find her own way and her own voice — with the benefit of an expert to keep her from going too far off course — in order for her to have ownership of her speaking programs and her business plan. I knew from Aunt Jennie's example it was vital she first try on her own. Only after she put information together would we make subtle adjustments.

An amazing opportunity presented itself: Shalini was asked to screen her film and give a presentation for an environmental conference hosting over 4,000 young people! Under my tutelage, she crafted a presentation focused on her challenge to the audience to become leaders, to find something they believe in and take action. She peppered her talk with references to her own life as an immigrant, an activist and a filmmaker.

STANDING OVATION

A few nights before the program, I had just retired to my hotel room after speaking at a convention of my own when my cell phone rang. It was Shalini and she was full of nervous energy and excite over her pending presentation. We talked through her program four times, making subtle tweaks here and there, until Shalini finally said in a firm voice that she was ready.

The day of her presentation I watched the clock, eagerly awaiting a phone call from her to report on her success. There was no doubt in my mind it would be a success: I believed in Shalini and more importantly, I knew I had helped her believe in herself. The phone rang in the late afternoon, and I picked it up to hear Shalini's voice on the other end.

"They gave me a standing ovation!" she said excitedly. "And they ranked my presentation as the best of the day!" I congratulated her feeling like a proud mother (or aunt!), and she went on to regale me with the details. Following the presentation, she was asked to present her business plan to an investment group specializing in media companies with a strong social message. She and her production company are on the way to success!

ON THE LOT

But that wasn't the end of Shalini's journey nor was it the end of our mentoring relationship. We continued to talk every week, setting new goals and reaching for new levels of success. A few months passed and I heard more exciting news from Shalini: she had decided to submit her film *A Drop of Life* to be a contestant on a new FOX reality show called "On the Lot" created by reality show guru Mark Burnett and filmmaking legend Steven Spielberg.

"I hesitated at first," Shalini confessed. "For a second there, I wondered if my film was good enough...if I was good enough. But then I thought, 'What would Michelle want me to do?' and the answer was clear!" I was touched that my influence had helped to propel this talented young woman into great success.

From the start, Shalini's goals were to advance her career and grow her business, but my goal as her mentor was to help her have confidence in her own ability. This relationship needed to foster a deep belief within her that she can stand on her own and trust in her knowledge and capabilities. If I had completed the work for her, she would never be independent. While I am working with her, I can guide her and expose her to different perspectives, tools and processes, but the optimal end result is she will no longer need my feedback (though she may still want it). This approach assures that in the future, Shalini will have the recipe for success in her endeavors that we created together to follow and make her own amazing "loaves of bread."

MBA (Mom's Business Acumen) Class: Guideline for Mentor-Mentee Relationships

You've risen to the top of your game and have established yourself as a great leader — now is the time to share what you've learned with those following in your footsteps.

Here are tips on how to give the most to the people you mentor:

1. Create an understanding of your and your mentee's deliverables up front.

2. Know what your mentee wants from the relationship: why has she asked you to be her mentor?

3. Respect each other's time:

    a. Honor your appointments.

    b. Make sure there is a regular set time to meet — consistency is very important to forward progress.

    c. Give whatever time you can, but don't let your mentee monopolize your time.

4. Create assignments and deadlines that will be of the greatest benefit to the mentee — and make sure she honors them.

5. Push your mentee past where they believe they can go.

6. Learn your mentee's communication style so you can communicate your insights to her most effectively.

7. Keep track of your mentee's actions that result from your guidance to determine if you are both going in the right direction.

8. Look for opportunities in which you can help your mentee and take advantage of them.

The mentor/mentee relationship can be powerful and fulfilling for everyone involved. Go out there today and find yourself a mentor to guide you toward the greatest success possible; or, if you're already a fantastic leader in your own right, share your wisdom with someone else.

CHAPTER 12

WHO'S IN *YOUR* KITCHEN?

CORTLAND AUNTS AND UNCLES

Despite having a HUGE extended family between the Shermans and the Yozzos, I didn't grow up with any local relatives. My closest relatives were two hours away. Instead, I had a community that my parents created from all of their relocated college friends. Because this group of newly graduated education majors all came to Long Island for jobs, they created a community out of common experiences.

No one had local family, so they all came together to help each other through the challenges of dating, weddings, new jobs, new kids, the toddler years, the trying teenage years, college hunting, daughters dating, and back to weddings and grandkids. We call this

Lipstick Leadership

"My mother taught me many things...mostly in poem form. Here is one of my favorites: 'Wake up early and do your chores. Count your blessings, the rest of the day is yours!' As a financial systems consultant, some of my work is tedious. I prefer the analytical work to the data entry. When I get tasks I dread done first thing in the morning, the rest of my day is easy and enjoyable. Mom is so smart!"

~ Julie Moore, Vienna

Advance your career with the help of Michelle's FREE e-zine. Sign up today at www.LipstickLeadership.com!

group the "Cortland Aunts and Uncles" and they were a part of our day-to-day support system. As close and valuable as any "blood" relatives, they helped shape me and my parents. Some were mentors, some playmates, some employers, some advisors...but the community supported the sharing of all of their talents.

SUPPORT FROM THE CORTLAND FAMILY

My "Cortland cousins" and I still gather to celebrate the Feast of the Fishes every Christmas Eve at my parents' home. The next generation of support continues as we help each other advance our careers, raise our kids, survive divorce, cancer, infertility, loss and wrestle with how we will care for the amazing parents we have been blessed with. This lesson of creating a community to guide and support me is one of the most important lessons that Mimi has taught me.

Last year, Mimi was diagnosed with Parkinson Disease and breast cancer. My Cortland family and the many wonderful friends that my parents have added to that collection actually fought over who would get to bring Mimi to treatments. She's doing great and planning on going on my book tour with me...that is, if I can pull her away from her loving friends!

Simple Truth from Mom:
Create your community...get support!

Now that you've met the women, men and children in my kitchen, think about who's in *your* kitchen. The next time you're on the phone with your mother, grandmother, sister, aunt or even your daughter, remember to listen to the pearls of wisdom and simple truths that could transform your career. It is by tapping into our available feminine communities that we can collectively advance our careers.

Lipstick Leadership

"As mothers, we teach by what we do and by what we don't do. Sometimes what we are exposed to propels us toward action, and sometimes what we wish we have propels us. I am the youngest child in a large family and by the time my mother was raising me, she was exhausted from the demands of the five of us as well as my father's illness. As a result, I became very independent and this drive continued through my college years as I balanced working as a waitress (to pay for college) with my full course load. This independence and ambition has helped me succeed in the corporate marketplace where the ability to work hard and remain focused has served me well. So thanks, Mom, for what you did and what you struggled with. It has

all helped me get ahead and become the successful woman that I am today."

~ Jane Wolak, Vice President of Retail Product Services, The Hartford Life Insurance Companies, Hartford

Submit your best "Mom's Wisdom" story at www.LipstickLeadership.com today!

COFFEE AND NEGOTIATION STRATEGIES

Last year, I attended a publicity summit in New York City where I was speaking on a media panel. I was helping new authors fine-tune their "pitch" to other radio show hosts and TV producers when I connected with a client also located in the city. To save a little time, we met at a coffee shop near the conference to have a last minute coaching session.

This client had been struggling for weeks with terms from a potential financial backer for her organic clothing line. As a young fashion designer with a few seasons of beautiful clothing under her belt, she was trying to launch her business globally. This required more funding than she had available...hence her dilemma and our coaching emergency. We had been working on the negotiation of terms for this partnership and how she would present her final position to her would-be partner.

After a couple of hours, she was ready. She knew what points she could bend on and what ones were deal-breakers for her. Being prepared to negotiate and knowing at what point she would either walk away or sign on the dotted line, she felt liberated. She wanted to celebrate her new-found power in this process — which of course, I encouraged! We headed out of the coffee shop and down the street to a local pub where she and her friends frequented for "happy hour."

CLAMORING FOR COACHING

As the crowd thickened, I began meeting some of this client's friends; some owned their own businesses and others worked in big corporations. After a few margaritas and a lot of chatter on our lives, they realized that I was the coach they had been hearing about from their friend. That's when the rapid-fire questions started...

"Michelle, you have nineteen and twenty year-old sons! How did you balance being a mom and growing your business, writing, coaching and the radio show?"

"Didn't you feel overwhelmed?"

"Who was the most impressive person you ever interviewed?"

"What was the best advice you ever got?"

"Do you have a mentor?"

"What can I do to get my boss to start to see me as management material?"

"I have a two year-old daughter. How can I stop feeling guilty at work for worrying about Grace and guilty at home for worrying about my deadlines at work?"

"Do you think balance is possible?"

"Why aren't there more women in upper management? How can we change that?"

As we discussed all of the issues on most working women's minds, we drew from not only my experience, but the experiences and perspectives of all of the women sitting around the table. We found solutions and sometimes more questions. In the end, we all felt connected and better prepared to meet tomorrow's challenges at work and at home.

Needing to catch my train home to Connecticut, I tried to make my exit. These wonderful new friends begged me to stay and offered up a place to "crash." They wanted more time and coaching! I promised that I would think about how I could give them more, and then I raced for the train to spend time with my family (without any guilt!). On the train ride home, I couldn't get these amazing women off my mind. I wanted to give them a whole community of advisors who understood their issues and were invested in helping them succeed.

Over the next few weeks, I challenged my team at the Cove Group to find the solution to working women's need for a mentoring community. From those hours I spent with my client and her friends sipping margaritas around a table in New York City to the brainstorming sessions my team and I had around our conference table, Mom's MBA was born.

My team created a community that has regular weekly access to my insights as well as the insights of the experts I know. Mom's MBA is a place to ask the questions you might not ask at work but need to know to advance your business or career, or if you're an entrepreneur, the questions you don't know who to ask on how to grow your business.

GET YOUR M.B.A. (Mom's Business Acumen) TODAY

Now that you have read about the lessons I learned from the strong women of my family and I have shown you how I took their lessons from the kitchen to the corner office, I have an important question for you.

Do you have a passionate resolve to become the leader you must become and create the life you have always wanted?

Imagine gaining the specific "know-how" that would allow you to grow your career to the six-figure mark or higher without compromising your most important relationships.

What if you could do it faster and with less effort than you ever imagined? It's possible....IF you have a mentor who can guide the way.

And because I am the beneficiary of so many great ideas from so many inspiring people, I have decided to donate a limited number of virtual seats to my "Mom's Business Acumen Career Growth" Webinar.

Yes, that's right! I have decided to donate the same material that the public has formally invested thousands in and offer this same opportunity and insights as my gift to you — IF you take action now.

These insights have provoked standing ovations from women in a wide range of industries and in every level of achievement along the journey.

Why am I offering this life changing webinar to a select few women colleagues at my cost?

Because there is a myth out there that teaches us we have to choose to either build a strong career or raise a healthy family.

The truth is, most women have been taught certain approaches around life advancements that just don't work. Therefore, most women aren't experiencing both a prosperous career AND a healthy household. So don't be hard on yourself if you're not either.

What I am going to do in this webinar is give you the exact same tactics I used to grow my business and allow you to reliably multiply your income every year just like I did. And you can do this while you double your time off!

For those who qualify I am going to show you exactly how to:

◆ Take advantage of the invisible advancement opportunities that are all around you that you haven't even learned how to spot yet.

◆ Create a working environment that becomes as flexible as you want.

◆ Gain rapid jumps in your income in man-dominated industries and business without compromising your integrity.

◆ Change the way you create opportunity to suddenly open a floodgate of new leveraged income.

What small changes in your communication can turn YOUR relationships from casual experiences with great people into a valuable support system for your career goals?

But the real key to your success will be this...

A 'mindset shift' that will transform you from a passive wage earner into an active career creator — with all the perks and freedom to prove it!

I am going to teach you exactly how to overcome your internal resistance to promoting yourself, develop a marketing savvy mindset, and quickly put into action brilliant strategies that generate the type of results you want and need!

This program will give you specific information, show you how to rapidly implement ideas, and motivate you to take the right action in your career.

Please do not apply to be a part of this career and life-changing experience unless you are prepared to fully and completely engage yourself in this webinar. This means coming to the table with an open mind and being ready to immediately implement and take action on the ideas that are going to be researched.

Truthfully, it is costly for me to build this opportunity for you without charging for it. But I am excited to do this for the women who are ready to advance their career while committing to take more time for their families. I will expect anyone who signs up for the program to share the same enthusiasm and commit themselves fully to the program.

The majority of people initially judge the value of a product by how much it costs them. I could easily offer the life-changing lessons you will learn in this action-packed webinar for $1,000.00 or more, but because I want to get more women from the kitchen to the corner office, I am giving you this gift. Since I am offering you this for free, I need to be sure you do everything to experience what it is worth instead of devaluing this wonderful gift I am giving you.

What's expected of you: When you register for the webinar, you commit to attend the webinar, complete your homework, and turn it in to me. I also want you to share your success story once you have quickly generated income from the M.B.A. webinar.

Stop reading right now if you are not ready and willing to commit to yourself and to me. I cannot afford to squander the limited seats available for this webinar on women who are not truly ready to change your life.

Honestly, I'm only seeking to give this gift to completely committed individuals who are totally devoted to feeling the financial benefits of taking their life and career into their own hands.

After you quickly generate income using what you learned on this webinar, I would like you to send me your testimonial with all the details of how I have helped you create the life and income you have always wanted.

Go to the following URL and find out whether you qualify for this offer now...

http://www.MomsMBA.com/KtCO

ABOUT THE AUTHOR

Michelle Yozzo Drake is the founder and CEO of the Cove Group, a management consulting firm in Mystic, Connecticut. She coaches executives and entrepreneurs in strategic communication, helping to improve their sales, customer service and their bottom line. She has a BS in Marketing and Management, an MS in Business Education, and over twenty years of business experience. When Michelle is not speaking or coaching, she can be found baking in her kitchen or creating in her art studio. Michelle resides in Stonington, Connecticut with her husband, Rich and two sons, Michael and Kevin.